Planting Flowers, Pulling Weeds

PLANTING FLOWERS, PULLING WEEDS

Identifying Your Most Profitable Customers to Ensure a Lifetime of Growth

---

Janet Rubio

Patrick Laughlin

JOHN WILEY & SONS, INC.

Published by John Wiley & Sons, Inc., New York.
Published simultaneously in Canada.

ISBN 0-471-03513-0

Printed in the United States of America.

10 9 8 7 6 5 4 3 2 1

This book is dedicated with gratitude and love to my husband, Al, and children, Jennifer and Scott. For more than 20 years, they have cheered my successes as well as suffered along with me the many difficult lessons I learned and have shared in this book.

It is also dedicated to my parents, who still ask, "So what exactly do you do?" Read on, Mother and Dad. It's all here.

—J.R.

This book is dedicated with heartfelt thanks, love, and admiration to my wife, Allison, and our three children—Barbara (a.k.a. Sissy), David, and Grant. It is only through their support, sacrifice, understanding, and encouragement that I have been able to spend so much time away from home. No words can adequately express my love and gratitude.

This book is also dedicated to my mother who continues to offer sound advice and counsel on a regular basis and whose encouragement is never ending. In addition, this book is dedicated to the memory of my father who taught me what it means to be a professional and more importantly, how to be a good husband and father. I'm still applying every lesson you taught me—someday I may even get it right!

—P.L.

PREFACE

No two gardens are alike. One gardener's flower is another's weed. The title of this book, *Planting Flowers, Pulling Weeds,* takes these simple facts and transplants them to the world of business. We won't attempt to tell you what your best customer and prospects look like, any more than we would tell you which corporate objectives would be best for you to pursue. But we do present a complete, integrated system for identifying and cultivating the customers and prospects that will help most in the pursuit of your particular corporate objectives.

We call our system the Direct Impact Growth System (DIGS). It was developed over many years of working with both successful and unsuccessful companies who operate in the most competitive and aggressive fields of business.

Planting Flowers, Pulling Weeds is organized into three parts, corresponding to the (a) planning, (b) execution, and (c) refinement of marketing efforts. Our philosophies are appropriate for consumer as well as business-to-business marketers and our methodologies address both online as well as offline marketing requirements. The techniques we discuss apply to strategic accounts or relationship selling, as well as transaction-oriented environments that rely on catalogs and toll-free telephone numbers.

In *You Need to Know and Leverage Your Customers*—we tell the story of Joe Amendola to frame a discussion about how evolving business conditions—tougher competition, compressing margins, new markets, generally inefficient sales, and marketing operations—make it valuable and, indeed, essential for you to know and leverage your customers and prospects to extract their maximum value.

Overview: It Takes a System makes the point that you can't know customers and prospects adequately or exploit the knowledge you gain without implementing a Market Management System. Our Market Management System has two main components—a Market Development System and a Customer Attack Plan. This chapter serves as an introduction to these elements and provides a brief overview of the 10-step process that makes up the main components of the Direct Impact Growth System.

Step 1: Defining Your Corporate Objectives begins the stepwise progression through the implementation of the business system that is DIGS. *Part I: Building the Value Segments* discusses a proven process for developing intelligent business plans and includes Steps 1 through Step 4. Step 1 describes the three most common approaches to setting corporate objectives, and delves in detail into the balanced and coordinated approach we recommend, using examples from Dell Computer, Mercedes, and others.

Step 2: Collecting and Storing Your Data gets into the nitty-gritty of finding, cleaning, organizing, and maintaining the all-important information about your customers and prospects that is the foundation of the Direct Impact Growth System. This is where many direct marketing books end, with the creation of the marketing database. But our Market Development System is just the beginning of the Direct Impact Growth System.

Step 3: Assessing and Analyzing Your Data continues the data-specific work with guidelines and tips on how to figure out what you've got, what you're missing, how to assess its integrity, and how to go to external information vendors to obtain information you may not be able to find in-house. We then discuss how you can apply the information within your Market Development System database to build and leverage powerful, long-term, and profitable relationships with your customers and prospects.

Step 4: Placing People in Value Segments is the most important chapter in this book. The Value Segmentation technique we introduce and analyze here is the key to figuring out exactly what flowers to plant and which weeds to pull in pursuit of exponential and profitable growth. It contains essential tools such as the Relationship Continuum and the Value Segmentation Matrix, and shows you how to use this vital information to ensure you can deliver the right message to the right client at the right time.

Step 5: Planning to Capture Value begins Part II of the book—Implementation and Execution. This chapter presents marketing pro formas, contact plans, rules for creating BASIC impact offers, and proven approaches that ensure your marketing programs tie directly to your corporate financial objectives.

We took away many helpful ideas from our tenures at Dell Computer, but perhaps none was so influential as the one we present in *Step 6: Organizational Magnification*. Organizational magnification is the multiplying effect that you gain when everyone in your enterprise is properly briefed, motivated, and focused on achieving your marketing and business goals. It's something we came to appreciate at Dell, and here we show you how to achieve it in your own organizations.

Step 7: Marketing Execution builds on the foundation we have established by putting our marketing plans into action. We discuss how to create and execute detailed work plans for mailing schedules, how to communicate specific plans for identifying target sites, how to generate and distribute informative lead reports, and how to design, develop, and implement integrated marketing programs and sales support materials that will inspire your sales teams into synchronized action.

Step 8: Sales Execution introduces a disciplined and professional way to approach your customers and prospects that we call *Structured Selling*. Our Structured Selling discipline fully integrates with your marketing efforts—aligns with your corporate objectives—and is compatible with any sales methodology you've adopted. We dissect Structured Selling into its major and minor components, from targeting high-value accounts to managing territories and tracking and measuring sales performance.

The last of the three parts—Evaluation and Modification—begins with *Step 9: Metrics.* This chapter stresses the importance of and provides guidelines for measuring and assessing six areas of your business's overall health: operations, market management, business health, opportunities, promotion histories, and response history.

A great deal of the potency of the Direct Impact Growth System lies with the way it is set up to always get better. *Step 10: Closing the Loop* discusses how to use real-time results of your current marketing efforts as feedback to enhance, improve, and modify future efforts.

Finally, in the *Appendix,* we identify a selection of books, periodicals, associations, and government resources you can use to supplement your specific implementation of the Direct Impact Growth System, and to suggest ways you can modify it to achieve your particular objectives. While we wouldn't think of telling you what to plant in your garden, or what goals to set in your business, we do take a personal interest in seeing that you have the best tools to help you achieve your aggressive business and financial goals.

JANET RUBIO
PATRICK LAUGHLIN

ABOUT THE AUTHORS

Janet Rubio has been working in the field of Direct Marketing for over 20 years. She has held senior-level marketing positions for major corporations, as well as running her own consulting company for several years. Janet worked for CompuAdd, a Texas-based personal computer company, where she launched and developed their catalog business. While there she also began the outbound telemarketing sales group. Each of these groups grew to $100 million in sales within the first year.

Janet then spent five years at Dell Computer Corporation, joining the company when it was a $750-million upstart and leaving it when it passed the $2 billion mark. She is responsible for leading Dell into direct marketing by launching catalog programs as well as targeted market segment programs. In addition, she built Dell's first marketing database, program measurement systems, and call forecasting models.

After leaving Dell, Janet worked as a consultant. Her primary clients included Mercedes-Benz of North America and Xerox Corporation. She developed databases and direct marketing programs for each. The relationship marketing program she designed for Mercedes-Benz won a Gold Echo Award at the Direct Marketing Association Conference in 1997. She founded Direct Impact, a direct marketing agency in Austin, Texas.

Patrick Laughlin brings over 16 years of sales, marketing, and database experience in the technology, consumer, and market research industries. Patrick was a marketing manager at Dell Computer

Corporation where he was responsible for creating, developing, and implementing numerous innovative programs that enhanced the efficiency and productivity of his segment's sales and marketing teams. These programs included SMART—the Sales and Marketing Analytical Reporting Tool—which provided detailed intelligence about customers and prospects and tracked Dell's performance against targeted accounts.

Patrick's experience also includes many years within the Ziff Davis organization, where he designed, developed, and sold primary market research solutions to major companies and assisted in the successful implementation of direct marketing techniques within several major telecommunications and high-tech organizations. Prior to joining Ziff Davis, Patrick worked for IBM in Winston-Salem, North Carolina.

CONTENTS

Part III
Evaluation and Modification

INTRODUCTION

The Need to Know Customers: Secrets of Joe's Garage

Your mailbox gets jammed with solicitations to buy things you don't want. A telemarketing computer interrupts your dinner to offer you something you don't need. You miss an important e-mail because of the unsolicited pitches crowding your in-box. Do these or similar efforts from sellers leave you asking yourself: Are my company's marketing programs similarly rejected by their recipients?

If that unsettling thought has ever occurred to you, then this book is for you. This book is about having a direct impact on potential or lifelong customers; it's about direct marketing in its full potential, redefined. We hope to provide you with a powerful, flexible, and effective way to offer your products and services to purchasers.

But this book is about more than that. It is about leveraging customers and extracting value from them.

Direct marketing offers businesses unmatched ability to deal efficiently with customers as markets, while retaining the ability to select just the right groups of customers to concentrate on as well as to leverage them and to extract value from them.

For all the promise and convenience of modern marketing, something clearly has gotten lost along the way. Part of the problem is that the sales professional, the one we knew and trusted—and who, perhaps even more importantly, *knew us*—has vanished behind an electronic Babel of call centers and mailing lists. Many of us can recall a different time and different methods. Whenever we're placed interminably on hold while trying to make a catalog order or each time we are confronted with a service counter employee who doesn't recognize us or, seemingly, doesn't know much about the products sold to us by his or her employer, it makes us wonder: Whatever happened to Joe?

Anybody growing up as Patrick did around Springdale, Connecticut, in the 1970s certainly knows Joe Amendola. Joe ran the garage on the corner, just across from Palmer's Grocery. Squat and swarthy, with perpetually banged-up knuckles and ill-fitting gray coveralls, Joe knew our family very well.

It wasn't hard, for instance, for Joe to notice the date of Patrick's 16th birthday. That was the day Patrick wheeled into the station in the rusty Oldsmobile Cutlass and made his first-ever request for a fill-up. Similarly, Joe could make a good guess as to when a customer got a long awaited salary raise and promotion that allowed him to upgrade to a newer car, or when somebody's parents were out of town and had handed over their keys to the family vehicle.

What good was all this knowledge about the people who frequented his garage? Joe pumped a lot of gas, certainly. Indeed, that was his main business. But he knew more and did more for his customers. After topping the tank of Patrick's Cutlass with high-test, Joe gathered more information. He got down on his knees and looked at the tires, running a finger over the worn treads. He popped the hood and took a long look at that huge Oldsmobile engine with its oil-caked valve covers and frayed spark plug wires. Two hours later, Joe totted up Patrick's first automotive bill. Tank of gas. Can of oil. A set of plugs. Oh, and one bottle of Orange Crush.

Joe may not have been anyone's idea of a sophisticated marketer, but he was, at the very least, an astute and natural salesman. He knew Patrick's mother by name, all the Laughlin kids' birthdays, and all of their driving habits. He kept scrupulous records of all their vehicles and knew when each one was due for a tune-up. And in the summer of 1972, when the Little League team he sponsored made the district tournament, nobody bragged more on the boys than Joe. It wasn't an act; he really cared. People brought him their business because he cared.

This was true Customer Relationship Management, something many businesses have tried and failed today despite the advantages of computers and the Internet. Even with his rudimentary tools, Joe knew how to analyze his customers in what today's marketers call *real-time*. When somebody pulled up in a late-model car, sparkling clean with new tires and windshield wipers—and, perhaps, a letter jacket from the local high school lying in the back seat, that tipped him off that it was driven by a local—Joe instantly recognized a good prospect. For a customer like this, Joe went the extra mile, checking engine oil and washer fluid and buffing those already pristine windows with a clean rag in addition to filling it up.

This extra attention meant Joe's customers and prospects often left with far more than a tank of gas: a set of tires, an air filter, a can of oil. As a result, they kept coming back, no matter if they bought a new car, or their old car was passed down to a new owner with a freshly minted driver's license. Furthermore, their friends and family came, too, having heard about the special service and attention. If Joe knew Patrick's buddy, Ray Murphy, had recently inherited a new-to-him clunker, he'd suggest to Patrick that Ray come down for a tune-up. In that way, Joe replaced customers who moved, quit driving, or died with new customers who were literally just starting.

What was Joe's secret? What captured such stellar customer loyalty? Most importantly and most in keeping with the subject of this book, how did he find more of the same types of customers who sustained his enterprise for decades? It all goes back to the same thing: The guy knew us, from maplight to lugnuts, and he leveraged his wisdom to find more prospects and to upgrade customers so they bought more from him. The supreme power of the ability to leverage knowledge of a market is what makes the Direct Impact Growth System so effective.

Joe didn't limit his knowledge to the Laughlins. He knew everybody living around us. In the same way a skilled direct marketer knows his or her markets, Joe knew his individual customers and the surrounding area's prospects. Because he knew us so well, he didn't have to use hardball tactics or strident advertising circulars. He didn't get locked into selling products at a loss in order to build market share. Even after cut-rate self-service stations sprang up, the Laughlin family and many others kept going to Joe's Garage. As long as he cared to stay in the auto maintenance business, we spent an ever-increasing share of our automotive budget at Joe's. Indeed, our loyalty extended even longer. Now, three years after Joe retired to Florida, Patrick's mother still gets her fill-ups there at his old station.

Joe Goes Global

By the early 1990s, Patrick had for some time given up earning gas money by peddling recycled golf balls down at the Sterling Farms Golf Course and was now developing a database-driven sales and marketing program for Dell Computer Corp.'s Major Accounts Division. Janet, who by then hadn't seen a pair of saddle shoes for longer than she cares to admit, was manager of marketing for one of the major divisions at the Texas-based firm.

Dell Computer was already a $1-billion-in-sales firm but it was still popping, more than doubling revenue year after year thanks to the vigorous employment of a business paradigm that would have done old Joe proud. Joe's knowledge of his customers and ability to leverage that knowledge to earn more of his customer's dollars meant he didn't have to rely on comparatively costly and inefficient mass-market advertising to sell his products and services. Dell's direct sales model meant it didn't have to trust its products to relatively costly and inefficient retail stores. Instead, Dell sold direct to customers. In a high-tech version of self-service gasoline retailing, it gave its customers the lower prices they craved by removing what turned out to be an unnecessary middleman—the retailer—between it and its customers. While Dell certainly didn't invent this sales strategy, it perfected it to a level never seen before or since.

In those early years, the Dell campus in Austin was a marvel of growth, its hallways crammed with new employees, its loading docks stacked with cartons. Computer magazines sang the praises of Dell's products and business publications regularly paid homage to the young visionary company founder, Michael Dell. Advertising? Sure, we had advertising. That's what made the phones ring. But with all the buzz surrounding Dell at the time, the computers practically sold themselves.

It was generally a wonderful time to be in business, especially the personal computer business. Even weak competitors were making money. Janet's marketing department at Dell had a $20 million annual budget and about 25 employees. And when they had an idle minute for reflection, every one of those employees was secretly calculating the worth of their stock options. They were going to be rich, no doubt.

But there were few idle minutes in those days. Communicating with other divisions, documenting the lessons they were learning, training the raft of new employees Dell was hiring every day—it all went out the window as they attempted to deal with a corporate growth rate that has few parallels in history. Still, Janet remembers one management meeting when Dell president, Joel Kocher, called for a rare moment of group introspection. He asked us to imagine what our young company would look like when it was mature, when we had built the greatest computer company in the world. He asked us to imagine ourselves when we were 99 years old, rocking on our front porches and looking back at what we had created.

It was a beautiful vision of the future. And it was great to be on top and on the road to ultimate success. But Dell's success and astonishing overall growth concealed some unattractive and potentially ominous problems. For starters, there was the home and small business division, which saw a loss in 1993. This wasn't just bad news—it was intolerable.

The problem almost certainly was not with Dell's computer offerings. People loved them. No, engineering wasn't the issue. Ultimately, all roads pointed to one place: It was marketing. We were selling blind, and we had been from the day we had opened our doors. Although we had a wealth of information about the people who were buying the computers (we were selling directly to them, after all), we'd never analyzed the information, much less put any of it to any real use. We had forgotten Joe the mechanic's one simple rule: *Leverage thy customers, every single one.*

Dell was not a place where flawed business practices were tolerated for long. We began rooting around extensively in the sales department's databases. After a lot of digging (and after recruiting some pricey East Coast marketing consultants), we finally got our first good look at our customers. To be honest, we didn't much like what we saw.

Disorder and Chaos: The Dark Side of Growth

What we saw was a hodgepodge of unsophisticated computer buyers and marginal spenders lured by word-of-mouth advertising and a scattershot marketing campaign. Sure, they had driven Dell's revenue rates through the roof, but were they going to be the ones who delivered rock-steady earnings growth further down the road? Clearly not. Many of them would not replace their machines as often as we needed them to. We didn't know that, at the time, of course, and we were spending millions in a futile effort to get them to update their machines every couple of years.

Another problem was that many of our new customers were computer neophytes. They tied up our technical support staff for hours with basic queries, which was costing us tons. Equally disheartening, these first-timers as a group were sending back their computers at a higher rate than the company's customer base at large. To our embarrassment, we found that we were allowing returns and granting refunds far beyond the stated time period for those exchanges to occur. That's how much we knew about our customers: We didn't even bother to check when they had become customers.

This was no way to run a gas station. It was as if Joe were giving special treatment to people who lived in another state and passed his station only once a year. Not only would these out-of-towners rarely buy more than a single fill-up, they would have been the ones most likely to leave towels strewn around the restroom. Not surprisingly, Dell's phenomenal growth slowed. But things didn't get truly bad until, about the same time, competition increased. The company's ever-surging stock price dipped. Our once-ebullient, if hard-driving, bosses suddenly got the willies. They gave us six months to clean up the home and small business divisions.

Those six months gave us a real taste of life in a pressure cooker. The knives came out in the office as people scrambled to protect their jobs. We saw a vice president put his fist through the glass of an overhead projector. We saw many gifted colleagues jump ship. Those of us who didn't leave the company got a stern comeuppance regarding this go-go new economy that people talk so much about.

To begin with, growth isn't everything. Indeed, rapid, inadequately managed growth caused many of the problems that we experienced at Dell. The home and small business division, which contributed about a third of the company's revenues, had actually been in an unseen, negative trend for a while. We had built the division's growth on a base of very occasional and extremely unreliable customers, very needy and unprofitable customers who threatened to pitch our company into a spiral of loss. We could never leverage them or get a bigger percent of their budgets, because they really didn't have any budget.

How had the mighty Dell Computer Corp. come to build a big chunk of its future on a foundation of sand? One reason is that, despite its reputation as an innovative direct marketer, Dell fundamentally operated the way companies had always operated. That is, the sales department sold product and the marketing department concocted ad campaigns. Rarely did the twain meet. The two departments operated under separate directors with separate budgets. Indeed, every department in the company seemed to be doing things differently. Nobody kept track of the costs associated with attracting customers. Everybody was out doing his or her own thing. We were a much-admired, very modern company operating under 1960s-style business principles.

There is a happy ending. While there, we participated as Dell refined some truly powerful marketing tools that allowed the company to right its ship. The company thrived throughout the 1990s largely because they quickly employed several elements of what has now become the system that we're touting in this book. Other firms ignored these principles or were unaware of them. They have not been so fortunate.

Scary Stories, Mysterious Problems

During her early marketing career, Janet worked for a company called CompuAdd Corp., a closely held, rapidly growing Texas company with a business model similar to Dell's: low-cost computers, sold directly to businesses and consumers. CompuAdd went great guns for a while. In 1990, the company reported revenue of $515 million, a 29 percent increase over the previous year. But the good company went bad quickly. In 1991, the annual revenue actually dropped to $513.6 million. While some of that drop was attributed to a business spin-off, the warning was clear: The gravy days at CompuAdd were over.

Bill Hayden, the founder and chief executive officer of CompuAdd, started the company by selling disk drives out of the trunk of his Chevette. Hayden had great entrepreneurial instincts, but still found himself faced with flagging growth. In response, he decided to move away from direct sales and build a string of bricks-and-mortar retail stores. It's easy to say now that this was precisely the wrong move. Indisputably, it was a death sentence for the company. In early 1993, CompuAdd closed all 110 of its retail stores and laid off 600 people. Three months later, the company filed for bankruptcy.

The striking thing about this story is the way the vigor drained out of CompuAdd even as the company churned away, building a great line of products. Like everyone else at the once-thriving company, Janet puzzled over the untimely corporate death of a company that once had challenged Dell. She wondered: What had caused CompuAdd's growth to take such a sharp turn south? Was it a one-of-a-kind tragedy? Or did the experience point to a fundamental flaw in many companies?

In retrospect, a marketer armed with the understanding of up-to-the-minute customer analysis and valuation skills can diagnose that CompuAdd's repeat purchase rate collapsed. Its existing customers proved *not* to be long-term buyers of its products. It was unable to acquire new, better customers. Sadly, CompuAdd is hardly an anomaly. Big companies and little companies, promising companies all, beach themselves in the very act of selling great products. We've seen it happen time and again. And we know why it happens.

Companies fail all the time because they're selling fantastic products at great prices to the wrong set of customers. These customers are the wrong set because they cannot be leveraged, and they cost as much to support as other, more valuable, customers.

After attending a string of corporate funerals, we started to see that all companies are bound by a few simple truths regarding the selection and retention of customers. The basic pieces of our system began slipping into place. We've refined them while working as consultants with many well-known companies, such as Xerox Corp., Braun, and Citibank. We've also worked for many more modest outfits that you probably have not heard of—yet. But whatever the size of the firms and whatever it is they sell, the problems they face seem almost universal. We've heard them expressed many times, from many executives. It often starts with a near-hysterical phone call, and a nerve-rattling comment or two. Some samples:

- "Our business was growing at an unbelievable pace. Then in what seemed like one week, sales went flat. It got really scary when sales actually began to decline. How can double-digit growth dry up overnight?"
- "I looked at our books last week and thought I was seeing double. My VP of sales and my VP of marketing seem to be spending money on identical programs. To make matters worse, they don't even seem to realize it. Our costs are out of control."
- "We just never thought about matching our product strategy with our customers' needs. We just assumed that we would add products as we felt we were able to handle it. Boy, are we paying for that strategy now."
- "We jumped into the one-to-one marketing camp in a big way. Since we didn't have a business plan, we spent thousands building a customer relationship management system that is essentially worthless."

Do any of these unfortunate outcomes sound similar to the complaints voiced in your company's offices and conference rooms? Do they resemble the thoughts that pop unbidden into your mind in the middle of the night? These kinds of problems don't just happen to dot-com startups. Some of our most troubled clients are also some of the biggest, grandest, and oldest companies in America and, indeed, the world.

In 1995, for example, one of Janet's first clients as a marketing consultant brought her in to help on a project for auto giant, Mercedes Benz, North America, now a subsidiary of Daimler-Chrysler AG. At the time, the U.S. sales division of Mercedes faced several problems: diminishing loyalty rates, a customer base with a rapidly increasing average age, and lack of success in its efforts to appeal to new customers. The fundamental problem was the company's inability to manage its customer relationships over a five-year cycle. The missing solution was a customer management system.

As Janet began deconstructing the company's customer base, she couldn't help thinking of the parallels with what had happened just a few years earlier at Dell. Like the computer company, Mercedes was being out-marketed by a new set of competitors. They had no infrastructure to stay close to its customers. Its customers had made a decision to buy an expensive car some time before, but Mercedes had done little to bond buyers to their cars since the buyers wrote the check. Loyalty is a fickle thing. If marketing and sales don't constantly reinforce positive decisions, it is easy for a customer to be attracted to an offer from someone new who is making noise in the market. Their current clients were defecting to Lexus and Acura, and the company was not attracting new customers quickly enough to replace the losses.

To be sure, the company was still making fine cars and its relationships with its customers were, in many ways, as high-quality as its products. Mercedes-Benz could have been leveraging those customer relationships and getting more from each customer as time passed. But it had nothing in its line that appealed to upscale image-conscious suburbanites who were likely to trade in cars every couple of years. A nimble upstart competitor, Toyota Motor's luxury offering, Lexus, was stealing these most desirable customers and leaving Mercedes with the dregs.

To attack the problem at its source, Janet designed a marketing program intended to build loyalty and draw Mercedes owners closer to their cars. Loyalty, as every salesperson knows, is everything in the sales business. But it's something that few companies much bigger than Joe's Garage successfully deal with on a corporate level. The approach Janet and the team took to changing this was to develop a profile of the type of loyal customer the carmaker needed to attract. Inspired by that map, Mercedes started a direct marketing campaign that was astonishingly innovative for such a buttoned-down company.

It began with a brochure mailed out to a group of customers. Then the company followed up by mailing disposable cameras to these same customers, asking them to take pictures of themselves with their cars. Using those pictures, the company planned to produce and send out picture books to the respondents. Expensive? You bet. But it really bound people to their cars. More importantly, it bound Mercedes to a very special group of people. The folks who sent back all of those wonderful pictures were absolutely in love with their cars and, as it turned out, they were the perfect customers to help Mercedes counter its Far East competition, evangelize to attractive new prospects, and turn its North American business around.

Magical Sales System Revealed

We wish we could report here that our Direct Impact Growth System is the result of a bit of effortless alchemy or maybe that it came to us in a dream. It would be nice to say we suddenly saw the light, that we developed a system in a flash, and that we then strode boldly through life making the world safe for capitalism. The truth is far more prosaic. Our system evolved slowly and through much trial and error. We made mistakes. So did our clients. Our suggestions didn't always yield fruit. Executives ignored our advice, and some fine companies died on our watch.

But the birth of our system can be traced to a particular time and place. The Direct Impact Growth System (DIGS) entered the world on a gloomy winter evening in March 1998, in a downtown hotel called the Grove, in Boise, Idaho. A new client of ours, Micron Electronics Inc., had invited us to give them a presentation.

Theirs was a sad story that we had, as marketing troubleshooters, become accustomed to hearing. We entered the tale just after the company posted a quarterly loss of $48 million, compared with $142 million profit in the same period a year before. It was the company's first loss in seven years. In response to this loss, the company brought in a new executive team including Chairman and Chief Executive Officer Joel Kocher—that same former Dell executive for whom we used to work. Joel wanted to develop a marketing system that would turn Micron's computer unit around, and he brought us in to build it.

A turnaround was clearly needed, especially in the marketing end of things. Company executives were spending upward of $70 million a year on advertising, but they may as well have shoveled the cash out a window for all the good it was doing them. Micron had a national consumer awareness rating of only 12 percent, a very poor mark for a company with a $70-million annual ad budget. Worse, Micron, which had a reputation for building high-performance computers and backing them with excellent technical support, was scraping by with a mere 2 percent share of the personal computer market. Mr. Kocher hired us to develop an integrated sales and marketing program that would grow the customer base as well as increase its value. We arrived on a snowy afternoon and went straight to the hotel where we were staying. Over dinner we scripted our presentation. It was good, but it wasn't great.

But that night, something clicked. As Janet sat at the little desk in her hotel room and Patrick reclined on the floor, a sort of vision of our system came to us. Imagine the scene: Outside, snow was whipping across the landscape. Inside, the place looked like a college dorm at exam time with papers, overhead transparencies, and empty coffee cups scattered about. We were rumpled, road-whipped, and anxious. Then our previously disjointed lecture about databases, direct marketing, and mass customization distilled itself into a logical, self-contained, step-by-step procedure for managing prospects, customers, relationships, and markets. Excited, we bent over our laptops developing slides. A few hours later, we rushed out into the snow in search of an all-night copy center. At 4:30 A.M., we stumbled back to our hotel rooms, exhausted.

About 30 minutes into the next morning's presentation, we knew we had the thing nailed. Both the vice president of sales and the vice president of marketing were leaning forward in their chairs with rapt attention. They saw the vision. When the meeting broke up, both executives scurried off to meet with their staffs. A week later, we were sitting in Mr. Kocher's office, and he gave us the word: Full steam ahead. We remained at Micron for two years.

Alas, this story does not end happily. Micron waded into systematic market management with a reasonable level of commitment. But after an initial jump in profits, Micron reverted to its old habits, which eventually drove it completely out of the personal computer business. Top executives valued the system and implemented major parts of it, but management changes kept things in turmoil and, without effective leadership, enthusiasm for a process that may have been able to save the core customer base never trickled down to the staff and got into the company's organizational bones. As we always try to do when results are less than satisfactory, we looked for solutions. We found it in a system Janet calls *organizational magnification*. It's presented in Step 6 along with specific approaches to getting an entire company to focus on corporate marketing objectives.

Meanwhile, right up until the end, Micron continued to make mistakes. Janet, a one-time Micron customer, routinely received five copies of the same circular the company periodically sent out. At the time, she hadn't purchased a Micron product in years. Yet, she continued receiving five identical circulars in her mailbox every quarter. Is that leveraging customers?

We had come away from Micron with a system that grows the number of customers a company has and increases each customer's value. We know how to get our ideas to infiltrate, not just through the executive suite, but to percolate through all levels of an organization. For those that try it, the Direct Impact Growth System works.

Everyone's Doing It—Or Are They?

Our system is a close relative and friend of One-to-One Marketing and Customer Relationship Management (CRM). One-to-One Marketing is one of the hottest concepts in business today. Or is it? Almost everyone has heard the one-to-one theories of Peppers and Rogers in their book *The One Future* (1993), but has anyone thought to link those theories to their company's executive objectives? Many companies go through the motions of gathering customer information in the hopes of developing better relationships. But are many of them following through? More importantly, are any of them making money at it? Everybody's gathering customer information, e-tailers especially. But what are they doing with that information?

Forget dot-com companies for a moment and ponder some old-school examples. Consider Domino's Pizza. Pull that little sticker off last night's pizza box and you'll see that it's a computer-generated label with your name, address, and phone number printed on it, along with a delivery time. Somewhere in Domino's vast corporate database is a record of every pizza you have ever purchased from them and the time of day that you bought it. In that database is the insight Domino's could use to determine what nights you work late, what you do on rainy days, whether you watch the Super Bowl alone or with friends, and whether you like onions or anchovies. But did they leverage what they know? Let's put it this way: Have you ever received a special offer from them that was specifically tailored to you, the crowd-loving workaholic, the rain-averse anchovy-lover?

We're not picking on Domino's here. They're no different from most of the other businesses in town. The Randall's supermarket up the hill from our offices dispenses loyalty cards to its customers.

With that card, they record every purchase that you make. But what does the company do with the information? Be assured: Not nearly as much as they could. It's not a failing unique to this grocer.

Most firms don't know which customers to leverage. They probably don't really understand what their customers think of them. Without that knowledge, they will find it hard to extract incremental value.

The next time you visit one of those big tennis shoe outlet stores, consider this: How hard would it be for that store to determine the approximate age and gender of every member of your family? They probably have the information on their sales receipts: the size and type of shoes you bought, when you bought them (the week before the school year started, perhaps) and, if you paid with a check or credit card, your name, address, and phone number.

Now, pretend you're the manager of that shoe store. With a little staff training and bit of data manipulation, you could collect this information to determine which of your customers would likely spend the most money with you over their lifetimes. You could make an educated guess as to whether a customer is single and childless and buying one pair of cross-trainers a year, or shopping for a large family, making many purchases to meet the changing needs of a bevy of fashion-conscious teenagers. Then when the time came to plan the year's marketing strategy, you could make a choice: Who am I going to target here? Who would get the fliers and the attention, the childless adult whose feet stopped growing years ago? Or the proud parent of seven teenage boys? Put that way, there's no contest.

You could go further. With this sort of information, you could determine what kinds of shoes to manufacture in the following year, what sizes to stock, and how much shelf space to devote to various products. Such information could even dictate how you decorate your store. Will wall posters feature Michael Jordan or

Venus Williams? Perhaps your best customers should control such decisions.

Most differences between customers are subtler, of course. But what could you do with the customer information your business is gathering as a matter of routine? The answer to that question is widely unknown today, despite the fact that Customer Relationship Management and One-to-One Marketing are current business buzz phrases. Close behind them are some related concepts: Prospect Relationship Management (PRM)and Market Relationship Management (MRM). Market Relationship Management is about managing your relationships with the market as a whole, including your current set of customers and the remaining prospects. Prospect Relationship Management is about focusing on those prospects and deciding who to funnel into your Customer Relationship Management engine.

Prospect Relationship Management is a primary engine of business growth—you can only rely on revenue from your current customer set for so long.

Online commerce has put teeth into all these concepts. For instance, thanks largely to the Internet, all sorts of mass customization are possible these days. Likewise, the creation of a direct sales force as well as the creation of a direct relationship with the customer, once prohibitively expensive ventures for many companies, are now much more affordable. Just a few years ago, to give one example, it would have been inconceivable that a company such as idtown.com could exist. This Hong Kong seller of midpriced watches churns out thousands of different made-to-order timepieces by simply assembling them from common, interchangeable parts. Equally inconceivable, perhaps, is that a big, faceless car company like Daimler-Chrysler could allow you to select the color of your Smart Car before they finish manufacturing it. But that's what they're doing by simply clipping the body panels on the vehicle at the last minute. Taking the customization concept even further is

Procter & Gamble's new venture, Reflect, which sells shampoos and cosmetics that are made to a customer's individual specification.

What does a big conglomerate gain from tailored offerings? More profits, hopefully, in the long run, but also something far more valuable: a unique insight into what each and every one of its customer's wants. That is one way to extract more value. Whether Daimler-Chrysler and Procter & Gamble fully understand this is debatable. The Smart Car, a relatively new offering, is not exactly burning up the track with sales. While Reflect is enjoying early success, it is still part of a company that is used to producing a product and then attracting customers to it, rather than vice versa.

It Isn't Rocket Science

It's fair to ask how our system transcends the standard buzz about direct marketing and mass customization. The answer is simple: We're offering more than the cast-off bits and snatches of a marketing stratagem. We're presenting an entire business philosophy, a closed-loop sales and marketing system that starts with developing the right corporate objectives, and then shows you how to gather information, analyze customers and prospects, develop the plans and means to nurture the best, and get the most value from them, from cradle to grave.

The Direct Impact Growth System allows practically any sort of enterprise to develop a targeted customer list inexpensively by using a simple database. It then shows you how to determine your company's wallet share for each customer and how to expand the share you have. Our system shows you how to attract a lifetime customer set by synchronizing your sales and marketing efforts so that they perform like voices in a choir.

We'll show you how you can become the default provider for each customer, the first company they think of when they make a purchase. Finally, we'll tell you how to invest in each customer.

Your sales and marketing efforts cannot be a series of single, one-off executions. Your efforts must be well thought out, coordinated and evolutionary in that they build upon one another in a logical fashion. They must all be executed in context, in a systematic approach—and that approach is the primary focus of this book through the Direct Impact Growth System.

What we'll teach you are things that Joe, our neighborhood mechanic, seemed to know instinctively. But we'll do you one better: With our system, you apply those principles, not to a neighborhood or a community, but to a region, or a nation, or even the world.

We've boiled our program down to 10 steps, which you can adapt to your own enterprise. We'll show you how to effectively gather and use data in a retail, e-tail, or phone environment without being too intrusive or compromising any privacy policies, how to divine customer preferences without resorting to clunky product surveys and how to develop a direct marketing program that won't require you to mortgage the family farm. Better still, we'll show you how to think about your customers so that the products you design in the future—kitchen gadgets or financial services—will be immediate best sellers. It doesn't matter if you're running the local pizza house on the corner or the hottest dot-com site in cyberspace. This system will work for all kinds of companies and all sorts of merchants.

Companies fail for all sorts of reasons. Obviously, our system will not improve a fundamentally uncompetitive product line, nor will it save a company that sells seriously overpriced goods. Bad businesspeople who use our system will likely fail anyway, but for everyone else, we promise this: Our system will maximize the impact of your products on the market through getting more out of your customers. We promise this as well: The customers you target will be the right customers, the ones you keep, the ones who are in it for the long haul.

When we begin working with a company, we always tell the executives that their success depends completely on their commitment:

This is a comprehensive system. But as Patrick often also notes, "This stuff isn't rocket science." Most of what we have to say involves simple concepts and common-sense applications. The foundation of the Direct Impact Growth System is elegant in its simplicity. The process of creating it was far from simple. It involved work over many years with many clients, all of whom paid far more than the price of this book to learn the principles we outline in the upcoming chapters. But our extensive work in this field doesn't mean that these ideas are widespread. Indeed, despite advances in information technology and customer data acquisition, fewer businesses than ever are employing these tried-and-true methods of customer, prospect, and market management. That's especially true now that Joe has hung up his coveralls and retired to Florida.

Facts to Remember

- Direct marketing offers businesses unmatched ability to deal efficiently with customers as markets, while retaining the ability to select just the right groups of customers to concentrate on as well as to leverage them and to extract value from them.
- Leverage thy customers, every single one.
- Companies fail all the time because they're selling fantastic products at great prices to the wrong set of customers. These customers are the wrong set because they cannot be leveraged, and they cost as much to support as other, more valuable customers.
- Most firms don't know which customers to leverage. They probably don't really understand what their customers think of them. Without that knowledge, they will find it hard to extract incremental value.

- Prospect Relationship Management is a primary engine of business growth—you can only rely on revenue from your current customer set for so long.
- Your sales and marketing efforts cannot be a series of single, one-off executions. Your efforts must be well thought out, coordinated, and evolutionary because they build upon one another in a logical fashion. They must all be executed in context, in a systematic approach—and that approach is the primary focus of this book through the Direct Impact Growth System.

Part I

BUILDING THE VALUE SEGMENTS

OVERVIEW

It Takes a System

You don't know enough about your customers. You don't know enough about your *prospective* customers either. But don't despair, most companies don't. As a matter of fact, most companies realize this fact only when it is too late—just like the executive in the following story:

> In a 1997 television advertisement memorable for its mixture of emotion and business acumen, United Airlines depicted a grizzled company CEO telling his staff about a phone call he received from an old friend—a valued customer who informed him he was taking his business elsewhere. Upon telling his story, this executive handed out airline tickets to his entire staff with specific instructions to visit each of the company's remaining clients. The commercial closes with that executive reserving a ticket for himself so he could personally visit that old friend.

We wonder what this commercial would have been like if the commercial had gone on and the executive was able to leverage his knowledge of that long-time customer and extract even more value from him on his visit? What if he learned that there was a personality conflict between his old friend and the assigned sales representative? What if he learned that his competition was providing a free trial or that they were holding older products in special reserve to provide smoother product transitions for this client? What if he'd been gathering more information about this customer already?

If he had more information, the commercial would have been about solving a customer problem and hopefully resulting in a deeper understanding and a more loyal client. The further result might be a customer advocate who openly referred additional clients to this executive's firm.

How would the commercial have played out if this executive were even better-equipped to leverage this long-standing customer relationship. Would his opinion have been different if he realized that his customer—while perhaps well-respected and generating ongoing revenue for his firm—was actually costing his company money? What if he knew the one-off systems configurations this customer required, coupled with the free-shipping concessions and dedicated technical support representative they negotiated, actually added up to more money than this client was paying his firm. Would his attitude have been different? Would the commercial have been different?

Put yourself in tomorrow's staff meeting and ask yourself:

- Can your team provide you with a list of your customers ranked high to low by value?
- Which customers require the least amount of time to transition to new products?
- Who has the lowest support costs?
- Who uses the Web to place their own orders?
- Who purchases more than one of your product lines?

Unlike the simplified conclusion that the United Airlines commercial leaves you with—flying out to visit your strategic clients will solve all of your business woes—the real answer is in leveraging your knowledge of your clients so effectively that instead of losing them unexpectedly, you increase your revenues from them in a predictable manner.

The premise of this book, as you'll soon find out, is that your firm's fundamental issues may be resolved by evaluating the marketing approach that you are using to garner new customers. This process is not "one size fits all." Making an impact through your direct marketing efforts requires systematically applying a methodology to fully understand and motivate not just your current customers but your marketplace as well. It is crucial to maximize the value of every customer relationship while minimizing and/or completely eliminating the time, effort, and money associated with recruiting unprofitable accounts that cannot or will not provide any long-term benefits to your company. The weeding out process is an essential part of this system.

We hope to offer you more than theory, more than a list of obtainable goals. Street-smart techniques that have proven results and can dramatically improve your company's bottom-line will be shared. We do not limit ourselves to Customer Relationship Management (CRM) although we discuss this topic throughout the book and applaud companies that have CRM initiatives. But CRM, by definition, only addresses customers. Candidly, as all good direct marketers know—customers eventually go away. Solely paying attention to your current customers doesn't allow you to grow your company fast enough to gain market share. Customers, like our executive's old friend come and go and while they are in your fold, we advocate building the very best relationships possible and maximizing their value.

Companies need to be focused on Market Management Systems (MMS) that incorporate CRM initiatives with Prospect Relationship Management (PRM) activities as well. CRM only gives you one-half of the equation; PRM gives you the other half of the formula. This book is about combining these two halves to allow you to manage a whole market through a comprehensive Market Management System (MMS).

We are going to discuss the role that direct marketing plays within an integrated marketing plan and the specific components that make up good, solid direct marketing campaigns. We'll show you how to apply a meaningful discipline to deploy these components in a systematic fashion that we've labeled the Direct Impact Growth System (DIGS).

We believe that if done right, DIGS provides your company with a firm foundation for the future.

The Role of Direct Marketing

Direct marketing's role is to bridge the space between brand image and point-of-sale. Direct marketing allows you to control the image and the message you present to customers all the way down to the individual customer.

To see what this can mean, consider the case of luxury car dealerships. Take a look at a magazine ad for Mercedes-Benz or visit the Web site at www.mercedes-benz.com. Other luxury car dealerships also provide good examples of this type of advertising. You'll see many images and language on themes of luxury, elegance, exclusivity, and pampering with lots of personalization and attention to individual tastes.

Now, visit a local luxury car dealership. What you will find may be very different from the image the advertisements of luxury cars project. When you walk in, no one will come rushing up to help you. If you are not actually ignored, you will be subjected to a careful, if not a little haughty, visual inspection. It is as if you have to pass muster with the salesperson before you will be served.

This is an example of a common phenomenon in marketing: A brand image is negated by the customer's actual point-of-sale experience. This is a serious problem, since it means that the money you may have spent on advertising, publicity, and other forms of promotion to create your brand image may be completely wasted by unprofessional or poor service at the point-of-sale.

Direct marketing has an important role to play in branding and positioning companies and products and delivering messages that build relationships that allow you to extract maximum value.

Can good direct marketing solve these point-of-purchase issues? Probably not. At least, not entirely. But it can do a lot. A systematic approach to identifying and attracting the right types of buyers and courting these buyers with a consistent and appropriate flow of relevant messages, coupled with organizational awareness of sales and marketing efforts and an understanding of how customers and prospects should be handled at the point-of-sale—all these can go a long way toward making all of your individual client and prospect experiences positive. This leads inexorably to higher value.

In a nutshell, that last sentence describes the foundation of our Direct Impact Growth System. It's about business, and making the most of your business's opportunities by understanding lifetime customer value and return on investment as applied to marketing. To fully understand the power of our philosophy, it is important to get grounded in the fundamentals of direct marketing.

Understanding Direct Marketing

The Direct Marketing Association (DMA) defines direct marketing as "... an interactive system of marketing which uses one or more advertising media to effect a measurable response and/or transaction at any location." The definition goes on to say that a response can be in the form of:

1. An order (direct order),
2. An inquiry (lead generation), or
3. A visit to a store, Web site or place of business for the purchase of a specific product(s) or service(s) (traffic generation).

The *Portable MBA in Marketing* (Wiley, 1998) further defines direct marketing by outlining the three basic properties of any direct marketing campaign:

1. A definite offer is made.
2. All the information necessary to make a decision is provided.
3. A response mechanism is provided.

Let's look at each one of these properties in more detail.

A Definite Offer Is Made

Direct marketing is not image advertising. You're offering something specific for sale or requesting someone take a particular action. It may not always be an order. Sometimes direct marketing just wants prospects to visit a Web site or customers to agree to meet with a salesperson. A variant may include a simple statement to the customer that, "A salesman will call." In this case, the action you are looking for is awareness of the pending call.

But direct marketing always has a specific action. Businesses have to make money, and making money is all about getting customers to behave in a certain way. This is important to keep in mind, because you want to make sure you are clearly asking for the action you want.

All Information Necessary to Make a Decision Is Provided

If a purchase is the decision you are after, purchasers can decide on the type, quantity, and color of the items they want by referring to the accompanying marketing materials themselves. For an example of this, look at the office supplies or clothing catalog that almost certainly resides in your mailbox at this moment. Once received, the consumer doesn't have to wait for a salesperson to call and explain it all—although often the purpose of direct marketing is primarily to get a person to engage in prepurchasing behavior, such as scheduling a sales appointment.

A Response Mechanism Is Provided

You are trying to drive behavior, so you don't ask people to look in the phone book for "a participating retailer." Direct marketers make them clip a coupon, slap a stamp on it and order, or point and click to download that free sample from the Web site. That's direct marketing: definitive, informed, oriented toward obtaining a specific response. A vitally important effect of this response mechanism is that it allows direct marketers to accurately measure the response to their marketing efforts. This is highly significant. Direct marketing's response mechanism creates the most powerful tool in the direct marketer's kit: a database of information about customers and prospects, their specific responses to individual marketing initiatives, and their long-term value to your enterprise.

Along with these three properties, there are three principal rules to which all good direct marketers must adhere:

1. *Your message must be relevant.* This means that the message the target receives must cause the target to react. For example, if you're selling a product that differentiates itself with excellent after-sale service, your message should stress this fact because it supports your brand position and it is meaningful to the customer.
2. *Your message must be sustainable.* Good direct marketing involves responsibility. If direct marketing supports your brand image and product position, one-time, unrelated offers that do not establish or extend a customer relationship have no place in your direct marketing efforts. Successful direct marketers provide offers that they can support over a specific period of time. Direct marketing should not be the vehicle for "get-'em while-we-got-'em" sales opportunities. You are charged with providing the marketplace with something they can use to start or build a relationship. If you are emphasizing free shipping, be prepared to offer it for the product lifetime to any client that responds to your offer. More importantly, be prepared to offer it to a friend of a client who has heard good

things about your company from his buddy and wants the same deal his buddy got—that includes the free shipping.

3. *Your direct marketing efforts must be financially modeled.* Direct marketing gives you the ability to be financially responsible in the way you spend your marketing budget. No other brand-building or image-management tool can show you so clearly what return you can expect to get for your marketing dollars. We said earlier that direct marketing involves responsibility—it is every good direct marketer's requirement to establish pro forma that accurately forecast the sales and profits of your direct marketing activities. This doesn't mean direct marketing is inexpensive. It just means that you should be able to model how much marketing you need and properly determine how many bucks you need to spend in order to get the highest return on investment and lifetime customer value.

Putting the Direct in Marketing

The Direct Impact Growth System has special value to marketers, but if you're going to get the maximum value from it, you have to approach it in an organized, systematic way. Our approach is far removed from buying 30 seconds during the Super Bowl or purchasing two-page spreads in every trade journal servicing your industry.

The nature of direct marketing gives you the opportunity and even the responsibility to make as much of it as you can. You can and must, for instance, feed the right number and type of prospects into your sales pipeline if you are going to replace the customers you're losing with new ones who will help you surpass your corporate objectives. To do that takes a system, not just a good salesperson promising the moon, or a clever advertising campaign with innovative creative content.

If you've got one customer, with one contact point, buying one product in one version, in one way, you don't need much of a system to manage it. You already know what that person wants, so connect with them and when it is time for them to order, close the deal, ship the product, bill the dollars, collect the money, and repeat the process. You can stay on top of this market with the back of an envelope, a dull pencil, a personal relationship, and simple intuition.

But when you've got hundreds, thousands, tens of thousands, or even millions of customers, there is no envelope big enough, pencil sharp enough, or intuition profound enough to reliably get you through the day, much less the quarter. You can't have the same type of personal relationship with a couple of thousand customers. Simple math makes this a completely different situation. You're forced to make decisions about customers based on the drivers of your business. You begin to segment your market by examining behavior and opportunities. This act of triage may be based on *behavior*—who buys every quarter from you; may be based on *volume*—who buys the most from you; may be based on *profitability*—who contributes the most margin to your company's bottom line. This is the process of value segmentation, and while it's only common sense to do it, it takes more than common sense to make it happen. It takes data and it takes a systematic approach to collecting, maintaining, and using the information you gather. You have to avoid doing research and performing market segmentation that isn't actionable. Your knowledge of customers and markets must provide you with leverage to boost sales and return on investment.

These challenges apply to prospects as well as customers. You have to know which of your prospects are most likely to turn into your best customers. How do you make educated guesses about what to sell them, how often and at what volume? What is the best means for you to communicate with each one of them—what combination of phone calls, sales calls, e-mails, or direct mail will get them to convert and become a customer.

Conversely, let's pose an equally challenging question: What prospects should you avoid? How do you identify the accounts or individuals who will consume too much of your support resources or not buy often or in large enough volume to justify the cost of acquisition?

When addressing an entire market, your opportunities are bigger and so are your challenges. You need new tools to know, understand, and manage a market—one customer and one prospect at a time—within a larger framework. You need a Market Management System (MMS).

Introducing the Market Management System

A Market Management System is an integrated business system featuring a closed-loop sales and marketing contact system that delivers relevant messages to selected targets resulting in maximum sales and deepened relationships at minimum costs.

Those are a lot of fancy words. In essence, however, a Market Management System (MMS) consists of two main parts. One is devoted to understanding and developing markets. We call this component our Market Development System (MDS). The other component of our MMS is dedicated to capturing sales. This we call our Customer Attack Plan (CAP). Here is a visual definition of our Market Management System:

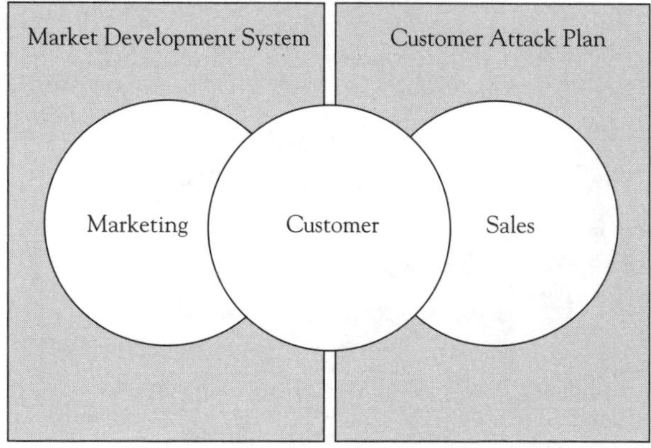

A Market Management System is customer- and prospect-centric and yet touches on and has ramifications throughout your entire organization. This is an important component of our overall DIGS system that we'll discuss in more detail in Step 6. We call this concept *Organizational Magnification*. Organizational Magnification is getting the entire organization lined up with the company's marketing and sales goals.

The Market Development System employs another important concept called the *Relationship Continuum*. The Relationship Continuum allows you to gauge your progression through the logical stages of developing a relationship with your clients. It is a tool that provides an accurate view of relationships and assists you in delivering messages that are appropriate to the stage you are in. It is a yardstick for measuring the percentage of a customer's budget you are getting. Visually, our Relationship Continuum looks like this:

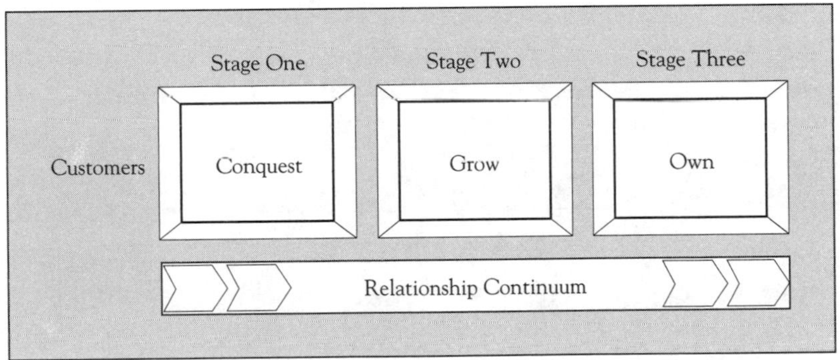

- *Stage One: Conquest* is the beginning of your relationship with a customer. At this point, you have little or no sales from the customer so you are clearly in the "courtship" stage of your relationship.
- *Stage Two: Grow the Relationship* is the stage during which you are increasing the amount of their available budget—share of

wallet—that you are getting. You might consider this the "going steady" stage of the relationship.

- *Stage Three: Earned Loyalty* is the position at which you have become the default provider to this customer. When they think of the product or service you offer, they think of your company first. At this stage, you have consummated the marriage and are living with the ups and downs associated with wedded bliss.

The other half of our Market Management System is our Customer Attack Plan (CAP). We will deal with this concept in more detail in Step 4. The Customer Attack Plan is a major component of another powerful DIGS subsystem called the Value Segmentation Matrix. The Value Segmentation Matrix is a tool for helping you decide which customers to go for first. It does this by segmenting your customers based on their value to you and on the phase of their relationship with you:

		Conquest	Grow	Own
		Relationship Continuum		
Available Budget	High	$$$	$$$$	$$$$$
	Medium	$$	$$$	$$$$
	Low	$	$$	$$$
		Low	Medium	High
		Wallet Share		

The details of understanding and implementing these business concepts and systems—Value Segmentation, Relationship Continuum, Value Segmentation Matrix, Customer Attack Plan, and more—are what the rest of this book is all about. The Direct Impact Growth System (DIGS) requires 10 steps for its execution, each of which will be dealt with in one of the remaining chapters. Here they are in brief:

Step 1 Define Your Corporate Objectives

There are three ways to define corporate objectives:

1. Top-down,
2. Bottom-up and
3. The DIGS way, utilizing both top-down and bottom-up criteria in a coordinated, intelligent fashion.

When you use DIGS to help you integrate the needs of investors and executives with the potential of markets and customers, you'll come up with targets that will be far more believable and achievable. They may well also be much more aggressive. Experiences with Dell Computer and Mercedes-Benz North America help illustrate the techniques for making this important first step in growth the Direct Impact way.

Step 2 Prepare Your Infrastructure

A primary building block of achieving corporate objectives is a database of customers and prospects. Building such a database is a challenging task but it can have a profound effect on your company's bottom line.

The process starts with ransacking your corporation's sales records, warranty card files, and service reports to identify the data you have on hand. The next step is integrating and standardizing salespeople's contact management databases, accounting reports, customer credit files, product repair records, and other data sources, often in incompatible formats, to make a single integrated database. You have to visit with leaders from every department to identify the individual pieces of information they have that you'll need to include within your repository to provide the insight they may require.

Prospects must be addressed in addition to customers. Since by definition prospects are not yet in your system as customers, this presents a different challenge. You'll obtain information about prospects chiefly from third-party information vendors. Identifying and evaluating these outside data sources is a key task in preparing your infrastructure.

You next design your database so that its contents can be accessed by the people who need it, in reports and formats that are easy to understand and useful. Along the way, you have to make sure your data can and will be easily updated.

Step 3 Assess What You Have

Now it's time to figure out exactly what you have. You need to identify what data is missing: Do you have estimates for customer budgets but not information on prospect buying cycles? You play out all of the what-if questions. Examine the drivers of your business and make sure you can answer all of the questions an executive might ask. Make sure you have defined all of the data fields that can provide the answers required.

Check to see that what you do have is accurate and complete and that it will be utilized by decision makers within the company.

Finally, look for and identify sources of data you don't have. Look for data that's better than what you already possess.

Step 4 Placing People in Value Segments

It's very important that you can categorize both customers and prospects on a value scale. At minimum, you must be able to place clients and prospects on a value seesaw—more valuable or less valuable. You must look at customers in terms of their lifetime value, their expected shelf life, their annual budget, and your "wallet share" of that budget.

This process of value segmentation is a key step in the DIGS process. Simple-to-use powerful tools like the Value Segmentation Matrix and customer profiling, evaluation, and placement—concepts that we'll discuss in detail—give you control over this potent concept.

Step 5 Planning to Capture Value

In this step, we'll introduce you to our version of a pro forma. The pro forma is a decision-making model that enables you to make sure that your direct marketing efforts will produce financial results that correspond to your corporate objectives. It uses simple, easily obtainable figures such as the size of your prospect market, the expected response rate, campaign costs, and expected revenues per unit to help you understand how many dollars you'll need to generate the reaction you were expecting.

Working hand-in-hand with the pro forma, Contact Plans help you structure and schedule the number and type of communications you'll make with each targeted account and prospect participating in your campaign.

Last but not least, we'll introduce you to a concept that we call *BASIC*—an acronym for Believable-Achievable-Sustainable-Interesting-Compelling. BASIC is a quickly grasped guide to crafting high-impact marketing offers that drive behavior.

Step 6 Organizational Magnification

Corporate culture is made up of many components. More often than not, employees in successful companies have a solid sense of what their company's overall mission is. Their articulation may vary, but the prevailing theme of what that company is trying to achieve usually is understood.

When employees are able to internalize the company's vision, they are much more apt to understand the importance of their individual performance in fulfilling that mission. Joel Kocher, when he was president at Dell, was a master at making sure everyone within the company had a common understanding of where Dell was going and how important their actions were if Dell was going to fulfill its mission. Communication is a powerful motivational device. Nothing galvanizes an organization like establishing a specific goal and communicating a specific plan of how that goal is going to be achieved.

Organizational Magnification takes the power of communication and applies it directly to your marketing efforts. Utilizing your Market Management System, you can establish and share realistic sales and marketing goals with every department within your organization. When done correctly, amazing dynamics start to occur—the whole company gets focused on exceeding your objectives, individual departments begin working as extended units, messages to your customers and prospects suddenly become clearer. Each individual within the company begins to understand and believe that they have a role to play in determining the company's overall success.

We'll talk about how these and other Organizational Magnification techniques get the whole company to focus on same corporate objectives.

Step 7 Marketing Execution

Your Market Management System establishes the foundation for your marketing campaigns. Now it is time to put your plans into action. We'll discuss creating and communicating specific work plans for identifying target sites, generating lead reports, preparing mailing schedules, and providing supporting marketing materials to your sales team.

A well-executed marketing plan is like a symphony. Each section of the orchestra has a specific role to play and a sound to share with the audience. The conductor must direct each of these individual units to perform in shared sequence to produce the desired music. Your marketing plans require the same discipline and sense of timing. Everything must happen in the right order at the right time.

Remember the old joke, "How do you get to Carnegie Hall?" And the answer: "Practice, practice, practice." Today's marketers ask, "How do you get your marketing team to execute flawlessly?" The answer: "Planning, planning, planning." Plan in advance and conduct regular updates with all concerned to see that they and their activities stay on the same sheet of music.

Step 8 Sales Execution

As we saw earlier in our luxury car example, the point-of-sales experience that occurs at the dealership can completely undermine a beautifully executed marketing campaign. Poor execution by your sales team cannot be tolerated. We'll discuss techniques and methodologies for preparing and communicating sales schedules, assigning tasks, refining target lists, developing scripts, preparing customer presentations, preparing correspondence, readying measurement, and tracking report templates.

These are the nitty-gritty details of Structured Selling—a sales methodology that is uniquely suited to compliment your direct marketing activities. Structured Selling is a system for boosting sales results by implementing four major components of a disciplined approach to your market—account planning, marketing programs, sales calls, and ongoing interaction. Set before a backdrop of specific territory goals and objectives established from your Market Management System, Structured Selling offers you an increased ability to leverage, manage, and measure specific marketing and sales objectives at the individual sales representative level.

Step 9 Metrics

You can't change behavior if you don't measure performance. Performance measurement is an integral part of the Direct Impact Growth System. We discuss the six areas of marketing that you should measure:

1. In *operations,* you'll measure the number of phone calls received, sales visits, floor traffic, number of Web hits, orders received, and similar items.
2. *Market management measurement* looks at numbers of new customers, spending rates, and numbers of customers lost.
3. *Business health indicators* include actual sales, order value, close rate, and more.
4. *Measuring opportunities* involves metrics for customers buying one product or more than one, one category or more than one, and so on.
5. To quantify *promotional history,* gauge promotional costs, times, and methods.

6. Finally, *response history* shows which campaigns people responded to, their method of contact, methods of payment, and other measures.

Step 10 Closing the Loop

Measuring for measurement's sake is not a productive task. One of the most potent features of the Direct Impact Growth System is in the application of what you have learned. We'll discuss how you'll use the measured results of your marketing efforts as feedback to modify the very beginning steps of your ongoing marketing efforts. This applied learning can help you identify changes that need to be made to your Market Development System or your Market Attack Plan. This incremental intelligence may cause you to change the contents of your database, the structure of your sales organization, or refine the level of reporting you need.

Taking the time to understand and learn from the good, the bad, and the ugly of your marketing programs might cause you some embarrassment in the short-term but it will probably eliminate some potentially deadly mistakes in the long-term. A sound check-up and a good preventive healthcare plan is much more attractive than open-heart surgery performed by the vultures on Wall Street.

The 10 steps of the Direct Impact Growth System are simple. What could be more natural than to want to get the highest return on investment? In another sense, they are often exceptionally complex, both in concept and in execution. It's not always easy to get a troop of hard-charging salespeople to forego their individualistic styles in favor of a systematic and disciplined sales approach. You face challenges implementing DIGS, but whatever concessions you make or guidelines you bend, you'll still be closer to fully executing on your team's potential than you were when you started.

The most important fact about DIGS is that it works. Its elegance lies in its simplicity—everyone in your organization can grasp the concepts, understand their role and responsibilities, and understand that their performance will be measured. DIGS does things you can't achieve and produces results you can't generate any other way.

Facts to Remember

- Direct marketing's role is to bridge the space between brand image and point-of-sale. Direct marketing allows you to control the image and the message you present to customers all the way down to the individual customer. Direct marketing has an important role to play in branding and positioning companies and products and delivering messages that build relationships that allow you to extract maximum value.
- Direct marketing's response mechanism creates the most powerful tool in the direct marketer's kit: a database of information about customers and their specific responses to individual marketing initiatives.
- A Market Management System is an integrated, closed-loop sales and marketing contact system delivering relevant messages to selected targets resulting in maximum sales and deepened relationships at minimum costs.
- A Market Management System is customer- and prospect-centric and yet touches on and has ramifications throughout your entire organization.
- Organizational Magnification is getting the entire organization lined up with the company's marketing and sales goals.

- The Relationship Continuum allows you to gauge your progression through the logical stages of developing a relationship with your clients. It is a tool that provides an accurate view of relationships and assists you in delivering messages that are appropriate to the stage you are in. It is a yardstick for measuring the percentage of a customer's budget you are getting.
- The Customer Attack Plan is a major component of another powerful DIGS subsystem called the Value Segmentation Matrix. The Value Segmentation Matrix is a tool for helping you decide which customers to go for first. It does this by segmenting your customers based on their value to you and on the phase of their relationship with you.
- The pro forma is a decision-making model that enables you to make sure that your direct marketing efforts will produce financial results that correspond to your corporate objectives. It uses simple, easily obtainable figures such as the size of your prospect market, the expected response rate, campaign costs, and expected revenues per unit to help you understand how many dollars you'll need to generate the results you were expecting.
- Organizational Magnification takes the power of communication and applies it directly to your marketing efforts. Utilizing your Market Management System, you can establish and share realistic sales and marketing goals with every department within your organization. When done correctly, amazing dynamics start to occur—the whole company gets focused on exceeding your objectives, individual departments begin working as extended units,

(Continued)

messages to your customers and prospects suddenly become clearer, and each individual within the company begins to understand and believe that they have a role to play in determining the company's overall success.

- Structured Selling is a system for boosting sales results by implementing four major components of a disciplined approach to your market—account planning, marketing programs, sales calls, and ongoing interaction.

STEP

1

Defining Your Corporate Objectives

You got to be very careful if you don't know where you're going, because you might not get there.

—Yogi Berra

The point of this quotation, and the business theorists who argue against the efficiency of planning are clearly at odds. One camp says you have to plan if you want to control events. The other says it's a waste of time because you can't control events—you just have to throw yourself into the mix and respond to the challenge. We don't intend to align ourselves entirely with either camp. Instead, we recommend that you guide your efforts and that you stand ready to modify your goals and objectives in light of the key lessons you discover along the way.

Defining Your Corporate Objectives is the first step in the Direct Impact Growth System (DIGS). It's also part of the last step, for an equally good reason—Step 10: Closing the Loop, is about using the results of your implementation of Direct Impact Growth System. To fine tune corporate objectives, you need feedback on how those corporate objectives are being implemented. Both theories of planning hold some truth. You can't come up with the perfect plan in advance of events.. But we also think you can come up with a very good plan if you first make the best one you can, then learn about the influence of events by implementing it, altering your plan as you go along.

As applied in marketing at Dell Computer, this is known as the "Ready, Fire, Aim" approach. At its simplest, this involves coming up with a viable marketing framework, adequately researching as well as you can in a timely manner, and then deploying it in the marketplace, perhaps in a limited test, to see what happens. Then you take what you learned and try again. If done correctly, this is not a willy-nilly exercise. It is a proven approach involving applied learning to revise and refine your thinking. Experience shows that nothing changes one's perspective like a few rounds of live ammunition whistling over your head.

"Any business that is afraid of failure is doomed to be a failure." We don't know who said this but it sounds too familiar to be something that we came up with. And it reflects the realities of today's economy. Unfortunately, not many corporations allow their marketers to fully employ Ready-Fire-Aim, because their cultures are too tightly bound to the idea that failure is unacceptable. Corporate culture teaches you that if you are going to fail you'd better be able to show that you covered all your bases.

Corporations have an even bigger problem than the way they pursue their corporate objectives. Many times, they get off on the wrong foot from the beginning by picking the wrong objectives, ones that don't truly dovetail with their business interests, are unrealistically aggressive, or too conservative. This unfortunate result is built into the fact that corporations tend to pick one school of objective-setting and neglect all others. We, on the other hand, believe in a balanced diet of examining multiple perspectives and arriving at a set of objectives.

Companes commonly set goals using one of two approaches. They either set goals top-down, relying mostly in input from senior management and outside influences, or bottom-up. Each is valuable and individually each provides part of the answer. But when used in isolation, neither of the two commonly used techniques for setting corporate sales and profit objectives will provide optimal results.

Top-Down Objectives

The most popular method of setting corporate objectives for revenues and profits is the top-down method. The top-down approach starts with a set of goals that are established to meet the expectations of various nonmarket entities. Often these include Wall Street investors and analysts, who expect a company to post unachievable annual revenue increases. If you fail to meet these objectives, it can seriously hamper your ability to raise capital, as well as generating heat from the investors who have already backed you. These expectations, while imposed by outside forces, are very real and must be addressed within your corporate plans.

Top-down objectives are also established from internal corporate goals. These have a number of origins. Many companies have historical annual revenue growth rates or other financial benchmarks that current management is committed to maintain for the future. Some corporate objectives are driven by nothing more than hubris, as when a CEO or chairman declares a desire to achieve $1 billion or $100 million or some other figure in sales by a certain date.

Bravado, as a component of goal setting, is not necessarily a bad thing as long as objectives are realistic and team members are able to convincingly envision themselves accomplishing the goals. Nothing motivates commitment like envisioning yourself succeeding. Dell, for example, in trying to gain a competitive advantage, established a company policy to provide 24-hour, seven-day-a-week technical service to its customers. While there were plenty of meetings discussing this initiative and laying out what had to be done, the final plans for executing it had not been completed before the company placed an advertisement in the industry publications touting the new service.

Did this create pressure on the people who would have to deliver on the promise? Certainly. But it also created commitment. Nothing commits your team to delivering like communicating a promise to the marketplace. Dell's move may have been bold but the pieces were in place and the team was motivated to succeed—their objective was in concert with the company's vision of the future.

That wasn't the only example of this practice that is deeply embedded in Dell's culture. The company similarly committed to and succeeded in finding a way to install proprietary software on customer's systems that were still on the factory floor, order-by-order and computer-by-computer. These goals were set by managers, but they were in line with the overall vision of the company as a direct marketer of mass-customized technology. Dell people spoke a common language of metrics and performance that helped them understand how to achieve these very aggressive objectives.

No matter what the source of the top-down objectives, the process of trying to reach them takes certain predictable paths. Once the goals are set, management has the responsibility of clearly telling the rest of the organization what they are and how to meet them.

Top-down objective-setting provides a set of highly visible guideposts that become the framework for allocating corporate resources. If the marketing department knows that 15 percent revenue growth is the objective, that provides a useful guideline in deciding how to implement future marketing efforts. Smart marketers select specific groups of customers and prospects. They attempt to understand them in detail and tailor offers to alter their behavior in the manner required to meet objectives for revenues, profits, and products. Figure 1.1 on pp. 52–53 shows how high-level focus on corporate objectives filters down to affect revenues, profits, and products.

The top-down view provides direction but is incomplete. The flaw in the top-down viewpoint is that it often represents a mathematical projection, often void of real perspective. Consider the experience of Micron Electronics. In preparation for developing the annual business plan, mid-tier management spent weeks analyzing their internal information to understand past customer performance, salesforce productivity, and the role additional sales tool might play in accelerating their sales efforts. Factoring these and a multitude of other factors into their plan, the team created a revenue, unit, and margin forecast that they felt was a stretch but obtainable.

Meanwhile, senior management was feeling the heat of Wall Street and was compelled to establish objectives that would please Wall Street's analysts and the board of directors. Unfortunately, these two trains collided head on and the plan of mid-management was ignored in favor of the Wall Street analysts' plan. The results: Not only were Wall Street's expectations set too high but mid-tier management became disenfranchised because they knew that the plan they were now expected to carry out was unachievable. Word got out and good salespeople—whose training had cost $50,000 a head—began leaving in large numbers. The strategy of the whole company was undermined by poorly set objectives.

It is important for public companies to address the needs of their investors. These goals must not be set without adequate reference to the markets and to their own internal population. Otherwise, a company is likely to set irrationally ambitious goals that the salespeople cannot hope to satisfy and, equally bad, have no investment in. Unreachable goals set people up for failure, sap company morale, and frequently make things worse. It's not surprising that corporations who ignore fundamental facts frequently fail to meet top-down objectives or, in fact, to set practical, achievable objectives in the first place. Not surprisingly, under these conditions failures are frequent.

Figure 1.1 Top-Down Financials (Read across page)

Corporate 2002 Financial Plan

Corporate		Jan-02	Feb-02	Mar-02	Apr-02	May-02	Jun-02	Jul-02	Aug-02	Sep-02
Net Ship	Product # 1	19,500	15,600	15,600	29,328	23,462	23,462	33,384	26,707	26,707
	Product # 2	2,734	2,187	2,187	4,208	3,367	3,367	4,857	3,885	3,885
	Product # 3	593	474	474	902	722	722	1,069	855	855
	Total	22,827	18,262	18,262	34,438	27,551	27,551	39,309	31,447	31,447
Net Rev	Product # 1	$ 31,557	$ 25,246	$ 25,246	$ 46,840	$ 37,472	$ 37,472	$ 51,307	$ 41,046	$ 41,046
	Product # 2	$ 7,918	$ 6,334	$ 6,334	$ 12,090	$ 9,672	$ 9,672	$ 13,751	$ 11,001	$ 11,001
	Product # 3	$ 4,091	$ 3,273	$ 3,273	$ 6,331	$ 5,065	$ 5,065	$ 7,366	$ 5,893	$ 5,893
	Parts	$ 1,034	$ 828	$ 828	$ 1,681	$ 1,345	$ 1,345	$ 2,233	$ 1,786	$ 1,786
	Lease	$ 72	$ 58	$ 58	$ 134	$ 108	$ 108	$ 186	$ 149	$ 149
	Retail	$ 1,124	$ 900	$ 900	$ 1,681	$ 1,345	$ 1,345	$ 1,489	$ 1,191	$ 1,191
	Services	$ 720	$ 576	$ 576	$ 1,076	$ 861	$ 861	$ 1,191	$ 953	$ 953
	Freight	$ -	$ -	$ -	$ -	$ -	$ -	$ -	$ -	$ -
	Other	$ -	$ -	$ -	$ -	$ -	$ -	$ -	$ -	$ -
	Total	$ 46,517	$ 37,213	$ 37,213	$ 69,833	$ 55,866	$ 55,866	$ 77,524	$ 62,019	$ 62,019

Targeted Product Mix - Monthly Distribution									
Product # 1	7%	5%	5%	10%	8%	8%	11%	9%	9%
Product # 2	6%	5%	5%	10%	8%	8%	11%	9%	9%
Product # 3	6%	5%	5%	10%	8%	8%	11%	9%	9%

	Jan-02	Feb-02
Total Net ShippedUnits	6%	5%
Targeted Product Mix - Within Month		
Product # 1	85%	85%
Product # 2	12%	12%
Product # 3	3%	3%
Targeted Net ASPs		
Product # 1	$ 1,575	$ 1,536
Product # 2	$ 2,469	$ 2,398
Product # 3	$ 5,323	$ 5,115
Targeted Revenue		
Product # 1	7%	5%
Product # 2	6%	5%
Product # 3	6%	5%
Total Net Revenue	7%	5%

Region 1 -

Region 1 Atlanta Metro		Jan-02	Feb-02	Mar-02
Net Ship	Product # 1	447	358	358
	Product # 2	63	50	50
	Product # 3	14	11	11
	Total	523	419	419
Net Rev	Product # 1	$ 723	$ 579	$ 579
	Product # 2	$ 182	$ 145	$ 145
	Product # 3	$ 94	$ 75	$ 75
	Parts	$ 24	$ 19	$ 19
	Lease	$ 1	$ 1	$ 1
	Retail	$ 26	$ 21	$ 21
	Services	$ 17	$ 13	$ 13
	Freight	$ -	$ -	$ -
	Other	$ -	$ -	$ -
	Total	$ 1,067	$ 853	$ 853

Top-Down Financials: Regional plans set as a % of the overall plan based on prior years contributions and all other assumptions applied.

Region 2 -

Region 2 Boston Metro		Jan-02	Feb-02	Mar-02
Net Ship	Product # 1	223	179	179
	Product # 2	31	25	25
	Product # 3	7	5	5
	Total	262	209	209
Net Rev	Product # 1	$ 362	$ 289	$ 289
	Product # 2	$ 91	$ 73	$ 73
	Product # 3	$ 47	$ 37	$ 37
	Parts	$ 12	$ 10	$ 10
	Lease	$ 1	$ 1	$ 1
	Retail	$ 13	$ 10	$ 10
	Services	$ 8	$ 7	$ 7
	Freight	$ -	$ -	$ -
	Other	$ -	$ -	$ -
	Total	$ 533	$ 426	$ 426

Oct-02	Nov-02	Dec-02	TOTAL FY02	TOTAL FY02
32,455	25,964	25,964	298,133	85%
5,020	4,016	4,016	43,729	12%
1,048	838	838	9,391	3%
38,523	30,818	30,818	351,253	100%
$ 49,599	$ 39,679	$ 39,679	$ 466,190	66%
$ 14,076	$ 11,261	$ 11,261	$ 124,371	18%
$ 7,266	$ 5,813	$ 5,813	$ 65,142	9%
$ 2,549	$ 2,039	$ 2,039	$ 19,494	3%
$ 219	$ 175	$ 175	$ 1,589	0%
$ 1,457	$ 1,165	$ 1,165	$ 14,952	2%
$ 1,165	**$ 932**	**$ 932**	**$ 10,794**	**2%**
$ -	$ -	$ -	$ -	0%
$ -	$ -	$ -	$ -	0%
$ 76,331	$ 61,065	$ 61,065	$ 702,531	100%
11%	9%	9%	100%	
11%	9%	9%	100%	
11%	9%	9%	100%	

Top-Down Financials: Corporate objectives set based on expected growth rates, product mix requirements, projected average selling prices, Wall Street expectations and corporate strategy.

Atlanta Metro - 2002 Financial Plan

Apr-02	May-02	Jun-02	Jul-02	Aug-02	Sep-02	Oct-02	Nov-02	Dec-02	TOTAL FY02K	TOTAL FY02K
672	538	538	765	612	612	744	595	595	6,835	85%
96	77	77	111	89	89	115	92	92	1,002	12%
21	17	17	24	20	20	24	19	19	215	3%
790	632	632	901	721	721	883	707	707	8,052	100%
1,074	$ 859	$ 859	$ 1,176	$ 941	$ 941	$ 1,137	$ 910	$ 910	$ 10,687	67%
277	$ 222	$ 222	$ 315	$ 252	$ 252	$ 323	$ 258	$ 258	$ 2,851	18%
145	$ 116	$ 116	$ 169	$ 135	$ 135	$ 167	$ 133	$ 133	$ 1,493	9%
35	$ 28	$ 28	$ 39	$ 31	$ 31	$ 38	$ 30	$ 30	$ 353	2%
2	$ 2	$ 2	$ 2	$ 2	$ 2	$ 2	$ 2	$ 2	$ 21	0%
39	$ 31	$ 31	$ 42	$ 34	$ 34	$ 41	$ 33	$ 33	$ 385	2%
25	$ 20	$ 20	$ 27	$ 22	$ 22	$ 26	$ 21	$ 21	$ 246	2%
-	$ -	$ -	$ -	$ -	$ -	$ -	$ -	$ -	$ -	0%
-	$ -	$ -	$ -	$ -	$ -	$ -	$ -	$ -	$ -	0%
1,597	$ 1,278	$ 1,278	$ 1,771	$ 1,417	$ 1,417	$ 1,733	$ 1,387	$ 1,387	$ 16,037	100%

Boston Metro - 2002 Financial Plan

Apr-02	May-02	Jun-02	Jul-02	Aug-02	Sep-02	Oct-02	Nov-02	Dec-02	TOTAL FY02K	TOTAL FY02K
336	269	269	382	306	306	372	297	297	3,416	85%
48	39	39	56	45	45	58	46	46	501	12%
10	8	8	12	10	10	12	10	10	108	3%
395	316	316	450	360	360	441	353	353	4,024	100%
537	$ 429	$ 429	$ 588	$ 470	$ 470	$ 568	$ 455	$ 455	$ 5,341	67%
139	$ 111	$ 111	$ 158	$ 126	$ 126	$ 161	$ 129	$ 129	$ 1,425	18%
73	$ 58	$ 58	$ 84	$ 68	$ 68	$ 83	$ 67	$ 67	$ 746	9%
18	$ 14	$ 14	$ 19	$ 16	$ 16	$ 19	$ 15	$ 15	$ 176	2%
1	$ 1	$ 1	$ 1	$ 1	$ 1	$ 1	$ 1	$ 1	$ 11	0%
19	$ 15	$ 15	$ 21	$ 17	$ 17	$ 20	$ 16	$ 16	$ 192	2%
12	$ 10	$ 10	$ 14	$ 11	$ 11	$ 13	$ 10	$ 10	$ 123	2%
-	$ -	$ -	$ -	$ -	$ -	$ -	$ -	$ -	$ -	0%
-	$ -	$ -	$ -	$ -	$ -	$ -	$ -	$ -	$ -	0%
798	$ 638	$ 638	$ 885	$ 708	$ 708	$ 866	$ 693	$ 693	$ 8,014	100%

Bottom-Up Objectives

The other popular way to set corporate objectives is to start from the bottom of the organization and work your way up (Figure 1.2 on pp. 56–57). Corporations do this a number of ways. In one common approach, individual salespeople are asked to forecast their territories' potential for the coming year, providing best-case, worst-case, and most-likely case scenarios. Sales managers apply their own experience to these forecasts to create overall objectives by district, region and/or individual product line. Eventually the process reaches senior management where corporate objectives are set based on the combined individual perspectives of the people closest to customers. The mechanism looks similar to the top-down process, running in reverse.

Objectives set in this fashion have some advantages over top-down goal setting. They're likely to be more realistic from the standpoint of what sales is likely to accomplish. However, the bottom-up methodology is fraught with practical issues as well. In practice, sales may sandbag estimates, restraining their projections to levels they know they can achieve easily. They may overestimate their capabilities or a customer's purchasing capacity so that they can tell senior executives what they want to hear. Another factor limiting the value of these sales forecasts is that they are tactical, not strategic. Rank and file salespeople rarely understand subtle market shifts, competitive threats, and other strategy-level influences. As a result, a bottom-up goal will probably miss the mark due to lack of information if nothing else.

The problem is that a gap frequently exists between what sales forecasts as doable and what other factors, ranging from investor sentiment to the CEO's personal agenda, consider essential.

In the mid-1990s, Janet was asked to help Mercedes-Benz with a relationship marketing program for its North American customers. The development portion of the project required six months of collecting and analyzing data about dealers, customers, and prospects. We presented our research and our campaign recommendations in a conference room in the Grace Building in New York City to a roomful of representatives from Mercedes-Benz headquarters in Germany. The presentation took over four hours. At the end, one German executive inquired, "So when all is said and done, we're going to sell more cars?" We nodded, pleased that the increase in unit sales we projected, on the order of 300 or 400 more new cars per year, had apparently caught his interest.

But the Mercedes-Benz executive wasn't nodding. He was shaking his head. "You don't understand," he explained. "We don't have 300 more cars." It turned out that Stuttgart had no idea that this relationship-building program would actually generate more sales. It never seemed to have occurred to them that they could control the business through marketing. The objective was to keep their image up, not to sell cars. To them, relationship-building was about brand image. They didn't get that it would drive sales.

Our experience with Mercedes-Benz is a classic example of taking a bottom-up approach to setting objectives. There was a huge information gap that we knew nothing about. The North American organization wanted to increase revenues and profits, so they pressed for a marketing program that would address these objectives. Without input from headquarters, which knew about the supply issue, the dealer objectives we had addressed in our project were invalid. Had we blindly executed on the campaign, we probably would have been successful in creating demand and customer satisfaction problems by not being able to deliver the cars. Talk about worst-case scenarios!

Combining Bottom-Up and Top-Down Objectives

Fortunately there is a happy medium that can be used to set corporate objectives. It includes elements of both the top-down and bottom-up approaches and we believe it is the best all-around

Figure 1.2 Bottom-Up Financials: Individual Sales Forecasts Are Rolled Up into Regional Forecasts Which in Turn Are Totaled and Become the Corporate Objectives

Sales Team # 1 -

AE	*John Smith*
ISR	*Jane Doe*
Region	*South West*
Month	

Pre-Call Planning | Marketing Plays | Customer Calls | Ongoing Interactions

				"STRUCTURED SELLING" CYCLE SUMMARY					PRODUCT			
Team	Customer	Value Segment Quad	Run Rate New Bus	A	B	C	D	Confidence Factor	Product	Qty	ASP	Total
JSJD	Aramark Services	5	N	x	x	x	x	3	Prod # 1	1000	1536	
JSJD	Kennestone Health	3	R	x	x	x	x	5	Prod # 1	100	1575	
JSJD	Norfolk Steamengines	4	R			x	x	4	Prod # 3	3	5323	
JSJD	Baptist Hospital	6	N			x	x	2	Prod # 2	28	2469	
JSJD	Mainstreet Medical	7	N	x	x	x	x	4	Prod # 2	17	2469	
JSJD	Northside Pharmacy	6	R	x		x	x	4	Prod # 1	25	1536	

									PRODUCT			
Annual Quota (SK)	YTD Actual	Quarter Quota	QTD Actual	A	B	C	D	Confidence Factor	Product	Qty	ASP ($K)	
				"Structured Selling" Cycle Summary						1173		$

Sales Team # 2 -

AE	*Amy Stark*
ISR	*Mike Angel*
Region	*North East*
Month	

Pre-Call Planning | Marketing Plays | Customer Calls | Ongoing Interactions

				"STRUCTURED SELLING" CYCLE SUMMARY					PRODUCT	
Team	Customer	Value Segment Quad	Run Rate New Bus	A	B	C	D	Confidence Factor	Product	Qty
ASMA	Bunker Technical	5	N	x	x	x	x	2	Prod # 1	100
ASMA	Apple Financing	3	R	x	x	x	x	3	Prod # 1	60
ASMA	New World Maps	6	N			x	x	4	Prod # 3	3

									PRODUCT	
Annual Quota (SK)	YTD Actual	Quarter Quota	QTD Actual	A	B	C	D	Confidence Factor	Product	Qty
				"Structured Selling" Cycle Summary						163

Opportunity Forecast & Tracking Summary

REVENUE	MARGIN		CLOSE TIMEFRAME			FACE TO FACE CALLS PER WEEK					
Revenue	GM %	Total GM ($K)	Current Month	Current Month +1	Current Month +2	Wk1	Wk2	Wk3	Wk4	Total	Comments / Obstacles / Results
1536000	15%	230400	50%	50%	0%	2	0	1	1	4	Waiting on corp relo
157500	15%	23625	10%	60%	40%	0	1	0	1	2	Negiotiating discount
15969	37%	5908.53	20%	80%	0%	1	1	1	0	3	Waiting on budget
69132	24%	16591.68	10%	40%	40%	0	0	2	2	4	Reorg causing delay
41973	24%	10073.52	75%	20%	5%	1	2	0	0	3	Verbal agreement
38400	15%	5760	85%	15%	0%	2	0	1	0	3	Proposal w decision makers
0		0								0	

REVENUE	MARGIN		CLOSE TIMEFRAME			FACE TO FACE CALLS / WEEK				
Total $$$ ($K)	GM %	Total GM ($K)	Current Month	Current Month +1	Current Month +2	Wk1	Wk2	Wk3	Wk4	Total
1,858,974.00		$ 292,358.73	30%	55%	40%	6	4	5	4	19
		Position Versus Weekly Quota				40%	27%	33%	27%	76%

Opportunity Forecast & Tracking Summary

REVENUE			CLOSE TIMEFRAME			FACE TO FACE CALLS PER WEEK					
ASP	Total	Revenue	Current Month	Current Month +1	Current Month +2	Wk1	Wk2	Wk3	Wk4	Total	Comments / Obstacles / Results
1536		153600	35%	50%	15%	2	0	1	1	4	Negiotiating discounts
1575		94500	25%	75%	0%	0	1	0	1	2	Planning expansion
5323		15969	20%	65%	15%	1	1	1	0	3	President resigned

REVENUE		CLOSE TIMEFRAME			FACE TO FACE CALLS / WEEK				
ASP ($K)	Total $$$ ($K)	Current Month	Current Month +1	Current Month +2	Wk1	Wk2	Wk3	Wk4	Total
	$ 264,069.00	30%	55%	40%	3	2	2	2	9
					20%	13%	13%	13%	36%

technique for establishing financial goals. Our example here is Dell Computer. Its process of goal setting was responsive both to corporate objectives and to market realities.

When it came to the bottom-up portion of its objective-setting process, Dell leveraged its extensive database of information of customer behavior. Analyzing this information, Dell was able to assign a value to each of its customers. Calculating changes in customer behavior, Dell was able to establish far more reachable goals than Micron. These goals were not necessarily more modest than Micron's. In fact, the reverse was often true. They were more practical, however, because they reflected a greater understanding of the mechanics of Dell's markets and the levers that controlled their business.

Dell didn't stop there. Rather than simply extrapolate purchase rates, the company used a market management system to identify and analyze the customers and prospects that could accelerate or inhibit its growth. Equally importantly, Dell was able to discern who, how, and when to activate their customers and prospects so the company could meet its objectives.

Consider a group of Dell customers identified by their placement on the Relationship Continuum as making purchases at a rate of $1,000 a month. By examining the information it had about these customers, Dell determined that they could be encouraged to increase their rate of purchase. By carefully reviewing sales records, customer budgets, input from focus groups, and other data, Dell was able to approximate realistic estimates of how much more these customers could purchase. Dell didn't unrealistically assume it could convince these $1,000-a-month customers to begin buying $10,000 worth of its products in an average month. Instead, they aimed to generate incremental jumps, encouraging purchase volumes to increase to $1,250, or $1,500, or even $2,000. This process resulted in objectives that were more realistic than a generic top-down process would likely produce. This discipline often resulted in goals that were very ambitious—sales quotas frequently doubled quarter to quarter—but they always involved a logical leap rather than a leap of faith. When salespeople understood how these aggressive goals were set, they understood also that they were achievable. That, plus a very generous year-end bonus and the stupefying performance of the stock options, motivated everyone to remarkable accomplishments.

Dell also incorporated top-down objective-setting methods, doing so in a particularly coordinated and intelligent fashion. Dell's corporate finance department realized that financial measures of its return on invested capital were significantly higher than those posted by other companies in its industry. To exploit this advantage, the company's reports to securities analysts began stressing the importance of this measurement—along with, of course, Dell's own superior performance in regard to it. This initiative was translated into specific goals and programs that encouraged and required salespeople and other revenue-generators to act in ways that would enhance the company's return on capital. Employing organization optimization techniques, Dell intensively communicated the concept, value, and methods of increasing performance on this metric to all its employees. This included a three-hour session on metrics, stock valuation, and competitors' position, plus a test to see how well the concepts had been absorbed. This balanced, self-reinforcing approach to setting corporate objectives, employing both top-down and bottom-up approaches, had a big effect on helping employees understand how their activities affected the company's performance and is one of the explanations of Dell's industry-leading record over the course of more than a decade.

Other companies can also benefit from such a holistic method of setting goals. When both top-down and bottom-up techniques are used to establish objectives, corporate financial goals won't be too modest due to a lack of industry knowledge nor will they be too broadly ambitious due to false bravado or external factors.

The key to filling the gap is having a market management system that allows you to evaluate customers and prospects, identify their potential for maximizing return, and develop techniques for tapping into that potential.

Only a Market Management System such as the Direct Impact Growth System fills the gap between bottom-up and top-down methods for setting corporate objectives that are both doable and worth doing.

A market management system enables you to understand your market, to know your customers—what they can do for you—and to help you reach your prospects. This sort of knowledge doesn't begin and end with a handful of airline tickets presented to a group of road warrior account representatives. It all starts with data—data about your customers, your prospects, and your market. Using data as a foundation, DIGS tells you what your customers want, what they can do, and how you can get them to do it.

Importantly, objectives set with the help of DIGS are set by the market. By combining DIGS with top-down corporate objectives, executives can zero in on goals that are imminently practical. If a group of customers doesn't exhibit the latent purchasing power necessary to generate the kind of sales growth that top-down agendas are going to require, then you know you're going to have to find another way. Given the penalties for missteps in an economy increasingly characterized by instability, forewarning is an essential weapon in any company's armory. If you spend much time trying to achieve the performance Wall Street demands but the markets—at least as you're approaching them—won't provide, you may well never get a second chance.

Perhaps you've been setting goals top down, with some input from the bottom of your organization, and you've done it without the help of a comprehensive market management system. You have been successful in establishing and exceeding realistic goals—yet ask yourself, are you achieving your company's full potential? You don't need a database to do top-down goal setting or to even do it well. But consider that Dell Computer's stock returned some 88,000 percent during the 1990s. No one was calling for that kind of return in 1990, and anyone who did would not have been treated respectfully. Yet, it happened. And it happened because Dell knew what it needed to do, what its customers and prospects could do for it, and how to convince them to do it.

Return to Micron for a moment. One of the company's primary problems in meeting its objectives was that its core customer base had significantly and fairly suddenly changed its rates of purchasing Micron products. What happened was that Micron had leveraged its reputation for building very high-performance systems and providing exceptional customer support into a very strong market position among engineers and other professionals who demanded the highest performance and latest technology available in the marketplace. This group, while loyal and enthusiastic, was limited in size. Lacking a foundation in the larger general market, Micron was fully exposed as its primary market became saturated and sales began to decline.

Customers change, so many companies have weathered similar experiences. However, Micron executives didn't know it was happening as it was happening. They only identified the trend after it had been operating for several crucial quarters. Scrambling, they launched an initiative to court the small and medium business market but dealing with declines in their core market while trying to build a base in a new market proved too much for Micron.

It's important not to be overly respectful of the market. Just because the customers you're relying on seem to be drifting away doesn't mean you have to sit back and take it. Dell was effective at tailoring specific offers that appealed to the high-value customers and targeted prospects that fueled their business. This ability, along with its direct business model, was the reason that the company consistently was able to gain market share. The company's strategy included limiting itself to no more than three main messages, typically one per product line. It kept those messages simple and kept sales and marketing people focused on clearly articulating the value proposition. Using intelligence from a robust database, it changed these messages every quarter to keep its perspective fresh and customer interest keen.

This type of coordinated, bidirectional process for setting objectives to the realistic maximum of the market's potential, then attacking those goals in ways likely to produce optimal results is not common even among the most sophisticated industries and firms. Xerox Corp., the unquestioned master of duplication technology and ruler of its industry, let its internal prejudices blind it to the invasion of Japanese copier makers in the 1970s and 1980s. This overseas assault was so effective that in late 2000 Xerox was capable of attracting rumors—incorrect, as it happened—that it was on the verge of bankruptcy. More recently, look at the way experienced businesspeople ran through millions, tens of millions, and in some cases hundreds of millions of dollars in investment capital trying to make dot-com businesses instantly achieve unreachable levels of sales and market share. Market management systems illuminate these blind spots, reveal the flaws in overly ambitious goals, provide directional pointers and guidelines that keep you on the proper path of profitability.

Now you understand the loopholes in the planning process. The next step is to learn how to build a database of market information and diagnostics to help you create your own market management system so you are not forced to act on impulse. After all, putting your foot in your mouth in front of Wall Street is just another way of losing your toenails!

Facts to Remember

- Companies commonly set goals using one of two approaches. They either set goals top-down, relying mostly on input from senior management and outside influences, or bottoms-up. Each is valuable, and individually each provides part of the answer. But when used in isolation, neither of the two commonly used techniques for setting corporate sales and profit objectives will provide optimal results.

- A gap frequently exists between what sales forecasts as doable and what other factors, ranging from investor sentiment to the CEO's personal agenda, consider essential.
- Only a Market Management System such as the Direct Impact Growth System fills the gap between bottom-up and top-down methods for setting corporate objectives that are both doable and worth doing.

STEP

2

Collecting and Storing Your Data

Every time you drop into your local supermarket, the cashier may ask you if you have the loyalty card the grocer offers to all its customers. The shopper in line ahead of us is surprised by the routine question and fumbles through purse or wallet for the little plastic wafer without really understanding how important it is to the store. With a swipe through the reader, the card transmits an array of information including the cardholder's full name, driver's license number, address, date of birth, home and business phones, and place of employment. In addition, the system records the items purchased. In return for sharing this information, the shopper gets special discounts on groceries, personal and payroll check-cashing privileges, membership in a video rental club, and the chance to direct a portion of the amount spent to a charity of choice.

Frequent buyer programs like this have become commonplace in everything from airlines to bookstores. In keeping with established practice, the grocery wisely promises to safeguard our personal information from prying eyes. It fulfills that promise, as far as we can tell, perfectly. But this supermarket chain also informs us that it will communicate directly to cardholders about shopper rewards, new product offers, newsletters, research surveys, and other programs "from time to time." We can opt not to receive any of this direct communication if we want.

Here is where it gets interesting: There's no reason to opt out of this service. The user never gets any mail or other contact from the grocery traceable to his or her participation in the frequent buyer program. In fact, being a member of this particular loyalty program produces no communications of any kind that we can see. Perhaps the company tailors its grocery offerings to reflect the purchase activities stored in its files. But we never receive any of those newsletters, certificates, announcements, or surveys they told us about.

From our perspective as marketers, they could do more. They probably use the information they collect for inventory management. Perhaps other arms of the organization use the information for other purposes. But when it comes to marketing, this company apparently doesn't know what it's got. That is a trove of potentially invaluable information for crafting offers, communicating with customers, and otherwise planting flowers and pulling weeds in its chosen markets. How valuable?

Collecting, organizing, and providing access to data about your customers and prospects is the foundation of the Direct Impact Growth System.

You heard right. Without adequate information about your customers and prospects, organized so you can use it effectively, you can't do the Direct Impact Growth System (DIGS). With it, you can do a lot, probably more than you imagine.

To get a view of how one company gathers and uses its customer information, consider Dell Computer. Any time you visit one of Dell's Web sites, place a phone order, or use one of the company's online support tools, Dell asks you to register and collects information about you. It also gathers information when you complete online surveys, participate in sweepstakes offers, request e-mail notifications of your order status, subscribe to newsletters, and interface with the company in any of several other ways. They gather the usual facts: name, e-mail address, phone number, address, and business type as well as information about your customer preferences. They pair this information with your order history, service history, and other data about your transactions. If you've never bought from Dell, they have a prospect database that they use to match you against and learn more about you.

So far, Dell's approach is much the same as the grocer. Here, however, is where their practices diverge. Using the information, Dell segments its customers into categories, such as ordinary consumers, home office types, small- and medium-size business, large businesses, special categories such as Internet service providers, and public entities like state and local government, federal agencies, educational institutions, and health-care organizations.

For each of these categories, Dell offers and delivers free e-mail notifications of special offers, updates, and other communications tailored to the segment. For instance, the Dell eNews electronic newsletter keeps Dell K–12 education customers up to date with news and events about product introductions, promotions, price changes, special offers, new customer programs, and corporate news. Dell has additional hard-copy communications with its customers, using catalogs tailored to product and customer segments.

The computer business is not the grocery business, and there are more significant differences between Dell Computer and our local supermarket than the way they gather and use information about their customers. But the premise of the DIGS is that it doesn't matter what industry you're in. If you market directly to your customers using DIGS, you'll come closer to Dell's average annual growth of almost 50 percent during the 1990s. The key to these benefits is the systematic gathering and intelligent use of information about your customers and prospects in an electronic database. So is database development all there is to being a high-impact direct marketer? Not at all, and *Planting Flowers, Pulling Weeds* is not just a book about databases. But if you're going to employ DIGS, you have to organize your market data in a systematic, detailed way that can only be accomplished by modern database software.

You don't have to spend a ton of money on technology for a marketing database. We've developed effective marketing databases for a few thousand dollars, using garden-variety Microsoft Access database software and scrounging cheap or free information from the Internet. Money is not the key. Advance planning, execution, and a sensible plan for maintaining a viable database are the keys to your successful implementation of our Direct Impact Growth System.

Three Fatal Mistakes Database Developers Make

For thousands of years in ancient Egypt, a written language was used to record business transactions, prayers, edicts from the pharaohs, and other communications. But during the period Egypt was governed by the Romans, this written language fell into disuse and within a century or so, the language was dead. European scholars puzzled for centuries over the meaning of the Egyptian hieroglyphics that decorated desert ruins and other artifacts of the ancient civilization. But it wasn't until 1799, when a French soldier near the Egyptian city of Rosetta found a chunk of stone bearing three clear bands of writing did these mysteries start to unravel. This famous Rosetta Stone was eventually used to decode Egyptian hieroglyphics and provide us with much of what we know of the builders of the pyramids.

Why are we talking about archaeology and linguistics? To make the point that no matter how big and robust your database is, if you don't set your database up properly, you could wind up with the equivalent of a dead language. That's not an appealing situation for a marketer whose goal is the creation of a database of information that is current, accurate, and appropriate to marketing requirements. Unless you have faith in your own ability to turn up a Rosetta Stone that will let you decode your own hieroglyphics, it's a situation you are better off preventing than trying to resolve it once it has happened.

We've encountered many marketing databases at customer sites, in addition to participating in the development of Dell's databases, and we've identified three serious errors businesses often make in developing databases:

- *Error Number One: They don't know what they are going to do with the data when they start collecting it and designing the database.* Typically, companies dump information randomly into such a database, without knowing what they intend to do with the contents. The thought is that they might as well build it for all possibilities. They can always pare it down later. This costs time, dollars, and equipment that can't be justified. Eventually, they may decide what they want to do with it, but by then they have often spent millions of dollars on a set of data that is out of date and not suited to their needs.
- *Error Number Two: They fail to come up with a plan for keeping the data fresh.* Something like 40 million Americans relocate each year, according to the U.S. Census Bureau, and the U.S. Postal Service corroborates that number by reporting that it processes about 38 million change-of-address forms annually. This is 15 percent of the population. If 15 percent of your customers move to a new location every year, after a few years most of the addresses in your database are likely to be out of date. Other information in your database is even more sensitive to the passage of time. You need to know *when* a customer ordered from you, or *when* you contacted a prospect. The only way to take care of the changing nature of customer data is to make plans to update the information in your database frequently and in a consistent fashion.

It is usually best if the data can be bought from a source rather than self-compiled. That way the data is consistent, available, and usually cheaper. Alternatively, the sales staff ends up having to collect data, and their time is better spent selling.

- *Error Number Three: They don't build the database with access in mind.* The information in a database is of no value unless the people who need it can use it to generate the reports and lists that they need. Unless you think about the reports you will need in advance, chances are you will get finished with your database and find it can't produce the reports you want because some key field is missing. Another element of access is making the reports available to the people using them. If you have many marketers who need to get into the database simultaneously, for example, you may need to put your database on a mainframe with many communications channels. Or you may want to make your database available through a company intranet or the World Wide Web. Failure to plan ahead can make these features difficult to implement.

  When we built a database for Dell at an outside service bureau on a mainframe, they charged us for every request made against the file. That is fairly common practice. Today, though, nonmainframe computers are fast enough to support millions of records and access is now easier. You want to make sure that you don't have to pay for each request because it will make you budget-constrained and you won't use the database for all it is worth.

Social Barriers to Effective Database Development

Even if you avoid these three common errors, there are some other issues in database development that will plague almost any person attempting to put DIGS in place. To begin with, the data about your customers and prospects is scattered. Any moderate-sized company has many islands of data. There are separate sets of data about customers and prospects in sales, in customer service, in technical support, in credit, and in shipping, just to name a few of the more obvious examples. That's normal and understandable. Accounts receivable may not care about where the products you sell are shipped so why should they keep that information?

Sales, on the other hand, needs to know where every product is. They will see their database content needs differently and will, by definition, build different systems. Frequently, they store the same information and then the challenges of data consolidation—taking both sources and bringing them together—and data synchronization—making sure that the data in each file matches—become tricky.

Social barriers to companywide database building are found in almost all companies. This is both normal and understandable. Often these systems and the data they contain have been bought and paid for by the individual department or division that uses them. They were not intended to serve the collective good of the company so much as the specific needs of their own organization. Few firms have an overarching policy of data collection that makes sharing of data a corporate mandate. If yours does, congratulations. If yours doesn't, you should know that you're certainly not alone. In any event, social barriers to effective database development mean that the ability to lead and manage people may be as important as information technology know-how.

Leading the Process

The process of developing, maintaining, assessing, and analyzing an effective marketing database is never ending and, clearly, nontrivial. It involves elements of database design and business planning as well as marketing and technology. It's not something that will happen by itself. So it's vital to firmly establish executive sponsorship of the effort.

Identify a project leader or data czar who is in charge of spearheading the effort. Make sure this cheerleader has a position senior enough to be able to push the project effectively and get people's ears as he or she explains to everyone involved how important it is that they participate.

Demonstrate why it is important to all participants that they execute their responsibilities. Require execution on all process steps, and hold participants accountable. This is a serious matter on which the future of the company may well hinge.

Any database-building effort has to be carefully led, monitored, and managed.

At Micron, this effort was spearheaded by Joel Kocher who gathered senior executives at the director level together for sessions overviewing plans, problems, and tasks related to marketing database development. We presented to this group for four hours, explaining the issues, outlining the mission, and demonstrating how the database would work to generate additional business. Kocher, whose title at that time was CEO and chairman of the board, personally took the executive leadership role and was briefed on an ongoing basis.

The information flow to help manage this project was highly structured. Weekly status reports were delivered to senior executives. Reports covered objectives, timelines, tasks, issues, and expected resolutions. It's important not to underestimate the challenge of such an assignment, nor to ignore the potential political landmines that may await anyone trying to build a database. Searching for data can unearth some unpleasant skeletons for some executives so be prepared for conflict, and don't expect the process always to be pretty.

One of the more significant challenges posed by developing a marketing database is in combining and integrating all the different sources of customer and prospect information in a company. To begin with, there are often many incompatible formats. Perhaps salespeople store their information in ACT—a contact management software—while manufacturing uses Baan enterprise software, shipping keeps its information in an old minicomputer database, and the e-business unit relies on SAP e-commerce software. Isolated storehouses of internal information are found to some degree in almost all companies. Translating the various formats into one that can be used in a single, integrated intelligent database is no easy task.

Incompatible formats is just part of the problem. Records gathered from different locations inevitably contain significant inconsistencies even when supposedly talking about the same group of customers. Janet may be identified as J. Rubio by shipping, but known by her full name to credit. How can we know these two names equal the same individual? Likewise, Patrick's residence may simply be identified by no more than his ZIP code in the marketing database, while customer service knows his e-mail, phone number, and cell phone in addition to his street address. Marketing may really want to know more about Patrick, but how can it collect all the customer service information into its database?

While it may be easy to reconcile these types of inconsistencies dealing with records in ones and twos, when you're wrestling with hundreds of thousands, millions, or even billions of customer transactions and other files, inconsistent data represents a serious obstacle to creating a useful database. This is not a small issue. It took a flow chart as large as a conference room table to code all the inconsistencies that occurred when we first pulled Dell's data together. In addition, as Web transactions mushroom, this difficulty is compounded. Not surprisingly given the challenge of customer data, Customer Data Integration (CDI) is a major thrust of the offerings of market information service bureaus, and one for which they are garnering millions of dollars from large companies trying to get a handle on their customer information.

Now turn your attention outward. No matter how much data you have on your customers and prospects, there is more information about them residing in external databases. Linking external and internal information can be even more difficult than linking isolated islands of in-house data. Differing formats, content structures, and other issues can keep your internal databases from

Figure 2.1 Consolidation Challenges

	File 1	File 2	File 3
Janet R	Age	Date of Birth	Age Range

absorbing the rich information available from outside vendors as effectively as an umbrella sheds rain.

In Figure 2.1, we show three customer files on customer Janet R. All the files carry the same information, however, they must be consolidated into one bit of information about Janet. The challenge of the information manager is to decide in which format he or she wants to carry the information.

Finally, it's always difficult to design a database to serve all the needs in an organization. Every department, sometimes every person, has a different requirement to make of the data. Look out in the parking lot and see how different vehicles are driven by the people in your company. Your people will exhibit a similar diversity of specifications in the demands they will place on the data you compile about your markets. It's probably not necessary for you to try to come up with the equivalent of a sedan-SUV-convertible-pickup-motorcycle when it comes to designing your database. One good strategy is to develop a relatively simple database that addresses at least some of the needs of several groups. However, as time goes by, you'll almost certainly want to add depth to reflect the diversity of your data's many users.

Common Database Contents

What kind of information is in a marketing database? The precise answers are different for every business, but generally the data in a marketing database can be grouped into four broad categories of information relating to (1) organizations, (2) competitors, (3) decision makers, and (4) relationships. Figure 2.2 depicts the typical type of content that companies may include in their marketing database.

First is data that aids you in understanding your customers' and prospects' organizations. To understand organizations, you have to know who they are and what they do. For consumer marketers, demographics and econographics help place consumer markets in organizational context. Company names and SIC codes are fundamental for business-to-business marketing. B2B firms will also want to know about their targets' organizational structure. This will include information about subsidiaries, divisions, regions, and individual locations.

To market effectively, you need to understand customers' and prospects' goals and objectives. Information about key dates, events, or seasonal influences that are important to the customers will also be very useful. Finally, you can gain insight into business organizations by identifying their key competitors.

Your database should probably include information about the competitive landscape as well, as seen from the customer's perspective.

Figure 2.2 Market Development System Elements

	Organizations	Competitors	Decision Makers	Relationships
B2B	• Company names • SIC codes • Subsidiaries • Regions • Individual site locations • Econographics	• Favored products • Product requirements • Favored suppliers	• Budget periods • Budgeting process • Decision-making process • Names of key decision makers	• Inside advocates • Political position • Relationship with key decision makers
	Organizations	Competitors	Decision Makers	Relationships
B2C	• Demographics	• Favored products • Product requirements • Favored suppliers	• Seasonality	• Influencers • Trend setters • Early adopters

Data should reveal: Whose products are they using? For what reason?

To sell effectively, you have to have a firm grasp on your customers' and prospects' purchase decision cycle. What is their budget period and process? Who makes decisions—headquarters or local managers? Can decisions be made by individuals or is endorsement by a committee required? How long does the decision-making process take?

Relationships are central to marketing, so your database should include some way of identifying any inside advocates you have in your targets. You should be able to record the status of your political position there and your relationship with the key decision makers. Consumer marketers may identify early adopters, trendsetters, influencers, and others whose relationships to your company may be important.

You don't have to organize your data by its connections to organizations, competitors, decision makers, and relationships. Exactly what you'll have in your database, and how you'll organize it, will depend on your market and your plans. Here is another way to look at some basic items that you should consider for inclusion in a business-to-business marketing database:

Essentials:

- Unique customer number or account code
- Company name
- SIC code
- Company size
- Contact name
- Job title
- Address
- Phone number(s)
- Fax number
- E-mail address
- Web site

Near-Essentials:

- The last time they bought from you
- How often they buy from you
- The size of their last order
- Their average order size
- How long they've been customers
- How you originally acquired the customer or lead

Ideally, you obtain:

- A budget for your product or services
- Decision-making power of the contact
- Budget cycles and key dates
- The percent of their business you are winning—wallet share
- How the contact prefers to be reached—by mail, phone, e-mail, or other means.

After you begin using the database for marketing, you'll have information about the offers made to each targeted customer and prospect as well as their responses. Keep in mind, the previous list is only for starters. You may have any number of additional fields you will consider essential for your database.

This is a soup-to-nuts description of the kind of data you can include in a marketing database. Many firms will find they need only a portion of these categories. Others will have unique needs not listed here. But you should at least consider these areas when deciding what types of information you will consider for inclusion in your own database.

Database Building Steps

Making a database that works the way you need it to may sound daunting or even impossible, but be reassured: Techniques for developing databases have kept pace with marketers' developing needs for them. There is a well-trod path leading from wherever you are to the creation of a useful database. We've led many companies down it and there's every reason to think you can follow in their footsteps.

Begin with a simple understanding: *The only customer and prospect data that is important is the data that your company needs to make decisions.* You can easily spend your entire budget gathering information nobody wants or can use. That's not going to do you any good. What you want is something people can and will use. To do this, find out what the people who will use the information think will be most useful. Then, prioritize your information needs. Finally, set expectations to increase the likelihood that your database will be accepted and used by those whom it is intended to help.

First, survey your audience. Ask them what information they need to do their jobs. Make it a *formal* survey. You'll want a clear paper trail showing that everyone was asked for his or her opinion in the likely event that complaints surface about the way the database was designed or implemented. Not that you want to shut off input at any stage of the process, but you want people to understand clearly that this is their chance to have their say and they should take advantage of it.

Use a variety of means for your survey. Poll some people with checklists and multiple-choice selection forms. Have others meet for focus groups to generate more open-ended discussions of necessary and desirable information. Collect forms and reports used by various departments in your company so you can go over them yourself to see what information is in daily use and what added information might be useful. Ask how and how often these reports are used. Ask who uses them. What decision makers are going to rely on these reports?

Second, when you've made significant progress with gathering information about data needs, begin a series of meetings with executive staff to prioritize information needs. You'll want to separate requests into two categories: information they *need* to have and information they *want* to have. These categories will differ by department and function, but what you'll try to end up with is an information scheme that will satisfy nearly everyone (as much as possible).

Third, it's important to initially set expectations correctly and manage those expectations throughout and beyond the actual roll-out of your system. Whatever you build will probably only get you to 85 percent of what you would like. Not everyone is going to be satisfied. It is important, therefore, that everyone feel as though their input has been heard and appreciated, even though their requests may not have made their way into the initial implementation of your solution.

Building databases is not for the weak of heart. It is a difficult and sometimes thankless task when the good solid work of cleaning data goes unnoticed. Rarely does the project proceed as smoothly as you would like.

Begin with the End in Mind

You've gathered and prioritized your data. Now it's time to jump forward to the end result. This is entirely appropriate. *When developing a marketing database, begin with the end in mind.* Think about what will be produced from this so-far imaginary database.

Don't limit yourself to recreating the reports you already use. Try to discern the level of confidence your recipients have in the information they currently receive. This sets your minimum threshold. Your reports must inspire the same level of (if not more) confidence as your current systems. Consider running parallel reports to verify the validity of your data prior to rolling out your reports to your constituents. Is your end-user missing anything? What reports or information do they want to have? What would they do with that information if they had it? For instance, are you going to want to use it to set corporate objectives? Generate leads? Follow up on marketing campaigns? Manage contacts for sales and service personnel?

Now is also a good time to ask if two or more reports can be combined. In database design, there is always a critical balance between providing all the information and options anyone could possibly want and risking overwhelming users with unnecessary complexity that adds only marginal value. So while you're trying to identify everything you should include in your database, remain open to reducing complexity as well. Cutting out or combining a few reports is something that you may want to consider as a value add-on for your internal or external clients.

A critical concern is that you provide ways to track marketing campaigns and measure the opportunities they generate. Think about what you want to track—Web site visits, requests for brochures, close rates, and so on—and how you'll track these items. This will help ensure that the systems, fields, and processes you will need for tracking response activity are in place. *Don't skip this step.* We have seen many an effort go awry when the focus on data overshadowed the requirements to measure and report results. If you don't consider what results need to be reported on from the beginning, there is often no way to recover from your oversight. Don't let this happen to you. One of the most visible results of a database are the reports it generates. Consider those reports now.

Designing for Access

The question of who will have access to the database is of paramount importance. If certain reports are for use by specialists, format might not be as important as the completeness of the data presented. If some reports are to be used by many people throughout the company, those reports need to be easy to understand, even at the cost of reducing the information.

Access is also an important consideration for maintenance and updating. Who will have the authority to run routines to eliminate duplicates? Who will be empowered to update information? Who decides what data takes priority among duplicate sources?

You'll want to think about how information will be provided to those using it. Will it be printed and distributed as hard copy?

Faxed? Viewed only or mostly on a computer screen? Will information be distributed by Intranet and viewable using browser software? Will users need to run an analysis against data sets? Will remote users be accessing the information? All these factors bear on the content and appearance of the output. Don't neglect, while you're at it, to reflect on how often reports will need to be published and refreshed.

Data guides decisions, so you should think about the logical actions that will take place upon viewing it. These could be as simple as a credit department employee placing a check mark in a customer's credit file indicating approval, or it could be far more complex. Consider how integrated your database needs to be with your other internal systems. Linking or hooking into legacy systems can be an undertaking in and of itself.

When you've completed these steps, you'll be ready to prepare a profile or data dictionary of the information you hope to gather. This profile should then be presented to those who will gather and use the information for approval, prioritization, and/or amendment.

Data as the DIGS Foundation

Why so much study and crosschecking to decide what information will go into and come out of your database? If data is the foundation of DIGS, the data dictionary represents the architectural drawings of that foundation. It will include a data dictionary for all the disparate islands of data, from sales to support, in your organization. The idea is to establish a lowest common denominator of necessary database requirements that will serve as the cornerstone for making informed decisions about your marketing efforts.

The data backbone you are constructing is nothing less than the common language with which your company will begin communicating. It must be considered one of your organization's basic building blocks.

A vice president at Dell used to say, "Don't build a cathedral when a church will do." Ideally, you will be able to follow this dictum, winding up with an amount and structure of data that is compact and simple enough to use easily, yet comprehensive and flexible enough to answer difficult questions. For example, you should be able to produce marketing information for a large customer in aggregate form by rolling up buying behavior of all purchasers in that organization. Just as easily, you should be able to drill down into the details associated with individual sites within that large customer. If you are a consumer marketer, you should be able to produce customer segment profiles sliced in any number of relevant ways.

In addition, you should be able to see through definitions of job function and title that vary between and even across organizations. If the operations manager does the purchasing for one plant but the purchasing manager does it for another plant, your database must be smart enough to recognize this relationship exists and deal with it.

You will often need several varieties of the same information for a single customer. For example, your finance department will want a customer address to send bills to, while the shipping department will want to know where to send the product that is being purchased. The two may very well be different locations, with a single billing address and many ship-to addresses. While you're putting together your information on customers and prospects, you need to keep in mind all the various duties that your database will have to fulfill.

A suitable database can distinguish the information needed by employees involved in various marketing and nonmarketing activities, and provide exactly and only what is needed.

That's a gold standard, and a tough one to meet. But if you proceed in a stepwise manner and always keep the end goal in mind, you can create a reservoir of market information that can provide your company with a true competitive advantage in the marketplace.

Facts to Remember

- Collecting, organizing, and providing access to data about your customers and prospects is the foundation of the Direct Impact Growth System.
- You don't have to spend a ton of money on technology for a marketing database. We've developed effective marketing databases for a few thousand dollars, using garden-variety Microsoft Access database software and scrounging cheap or free information from the Internet. Money is not the key. Advance planning, execution, and a sensible plan for maintaining a viable database are the keys to your successful implementation of our Direct Impact Growth System.
- The most common mistake direct marketers make with their databases is that they don't really know what they are going to do with the data when they start collecting it and designing the database.
- The second common error is that they fail to come up with a plan for keeping the data fresh.
- The third error is that they don't build the database with access in mind.
- The process of developing, maintaining, assessing, and analyzing an effective marketing database is never ending and nontrivial. It involves elements of database design and business planning as well as marketing and technology. It's not something that will happen by itself, so it's vital to firmly establish executive sponsorship of the effort.
- Any database-building effort has to be carefully led, monitored, and managed.

(Continued)

- The only customer and prospect data that is important is the data that your company needs to have to make decisions.
- Records gathered from different locations inevitably contain significant inconsistencies even when supposedly talking about the same group of customers.
- The data description you are constructing is nothing less than one of your organization's basic building blocks.
- A suitable database can distinguish the information needed by employees involved in various marketing and nonmarketing activities and provide exactly and only what is needed.

STEP

3

Assessing and Analyzing Your Data

"Education is learning what you didn't even know you didn't know," said historian David Boorstin. The third step in the Direct Impact Growth System involves assessing and analyzing the data you have collected. In this educational process, you are quite likely to learn certain things about your customers that you previously didn't know, as well as find out that some of the things you thought you knew to be true were actually false.

In this chapter, we discuss two major items. First we discuss the accuracy and completeness of your database and, second, we discuss different tools and techniques for analyzing the information you have. The assessment phase has two major parts. First, you have to figure out how accurate the data you have collected is and where it needs to be freshened or corrected. Second, you have to determine how complete the data is, based on your needs, and what is missing.

Analyzing your data is a way to gain insight through data mining and modeling techniques.

Assessing Your Data

In direct marketing using a database, issues of accuracy, freshness, and completeness constantly come up. Let us give you an example illustrating how important it is to have current and complete data in your Market Development System. When a Micron direct marketing campaign produced less-than-expected results, questions were asked about the quality of the lists we used in the campaign. We retained an outside research firm, Intelliquest, to interview people at a portion of our targeted sites as an accuracy check. Intelliquest's telephone interviews and analysis found that almost a quarter of those individuals we had targeted were no longer with the company, while another 14 percent of the contacts were identified as "no such person or position" at the targeted firm.

That wasn't all. On further investigation, we discovered that many of the records we used were missing key data fields. Many others contained blanks in fields where there should have been information.

As a result, nearly half of our file was worthless. To make matters worse, we didn't find out about it until after the mailing had gone out. How could this happen? Quite simply, as a matter of fact. Micron felt that their customer file would be a solid source of up-to-date information. They were wrong. Bad data in, bad data out. Bad data doomed the campaign from the start.

Be warned: The work we are about to describe in this chapter is not glamorous. There are no award shows honoring individuals for their outstanding contributions in the field of finding mistakes, correcting errors, and analyzing data in the company's Market Development System. This is an effort that can range from merely routine to outright dull. Read on, however, because the information this chapter discusses is vital to your success as a business professional.

As difficult as the next 20 minutes may be, the time and trouble we may save you will pay huge dividends in the future.

When you put in bad data and do nothing to change it, you get out bad data. In DIGS, the most critical variable in determining the success of any marketing effort is not the cleverness of the copy or the power of the offer. The most important attribute of a successful campaign is the quality of your marketing data.

Good creative content is generally assigned only 20 percent of the credit for any successful marketing campaign. Even the terms of the offer are not more important than the database you use. Around 40 percent of the success of a direct marketing effort is credited to selecting the right group of customers or prospects. Keeping that statistic in mind as you go about ensuring the good health of your database may help keep your mind focused and your frustrations in check. Unenthusiastic as you may be—read on McDuff, read on!

Conscientious businesspeople, once they are made aware of the importance of fresh data, are likely to demand that all their data be as up-to-date as possible. However, data assessment is more complicated than that. Having absolutely current data is not always desirable or even feasible. For instance, should every sales transaction be entered in the marketing database the instant it is concluded? A marketing database doesn't require that kind of immediacy. Even hourly updates of sales transactions are likely to be more than a marketing database can justify. Examine your business requirements and put a process and refresh schedule in place that meets your needs in a cost-efficient fashion. Consider starting with daily or weekly updates of new customer records and new customer addresses received in-house as well as sales transactions by products and product lines. Monthly or quarterly updates are likely to suffice for updating a database with compiled third-party data such as consumer demographics or industry verticals on your business files.

The frequency with which data is loaded into your database isn't the only variable controlling its accuracy. There are many other sources of potential error in your data. As a rule of thumb, you can assume that somewhere around 15 percent of your data is somehow imperfect. What keeps that number steady in spite of marketers' best efforts is an array of powerful forces working to compromise the value of any set of marketing data.

Let's start with simple inaccuracies. If you have compiled your database from a number of places, such as different departments in your company, it is almost certain to contain errors due to the problems inherent in consolidating data from various sources. Recall that you are pulling together information from all sorts of formats and from all sorts of places: sales records, customer service calls, warranty cards, shipping labels, credit files, salespeople's contact files, and so forth. It's almost certain when you bring all this information together in one database, that some data will be missing.

Which missing data is important? There is only one answer to this question: The data you need to answer the questions you are asking of the database.

Typically, the questions you are going to ask are questions that relate to the individual or combined drivers of your business. If your business has a major seasonality swing associated with it, you'll want to make sure that you've captured purchase history information, down to the product detail in a manner that allows you to plot quarter-on-quarter and year-on-year trends. Sounds simple we know, but what happens to your trends when June 2001 has five weeks in it and June 2002 has only four—are you able to accommodate this type of fluctuation in your database and reports? If you want to find out which customers have spent the most with you over the last five years, you have to have dated sales records broken out by individual customers and locations dating back at least that long. Other questions your DIGS database is likely to be asked include:

- Which of your customers have the largest budgets?
- How much of their budget is being spent with you?
- How have they responded to past contacts?
- How have responses varied by the person contacted and the manner of contact?

Ask yourself the questions you will want to know the answers to for your marketing efforts. Then, pose them to your database. If the answers don't come back or don't test out to conform with predictions, you may have a significant missing information or formatting problem. Keep in mind, however, that the questions you ask are likely to change and evolve. So if you can envision the likelihood of asking a question in the foreseeable future, consider making it a requirement for your database.

Sometimes your database may wind up with extra and/or unwanted information. Unwanted data can make your database unnecessarily large and therefore slow in producing reports, as well as increase the cost of maintaining and using it. Excess data may come from several sources. Internally, for example, if you are merging shipping department data with sales transaction data, you may find the shipping records come with information about things such as availability of loading docks and pallet sizes used at customer locations. This information may be useful to the shipping department but not necessarily to marketing. You can use scrubbing software to recognize and remove extraneous information from your marketing database, increasing its utility and accuracy. Extraneous information can also come from external sources. An experience at a marketing information firm where Patrick once worked makes this point. This firm sold profiles of medium and large-sized companies. These profiles provided detailed information about what computer hardware and software these companies had installed or were planning to buy. The data contained in these profiles was gathered in a very disciplined fashion involving a series of comprehensive telephone interviews with decision makers at each site. A disgruntled market researcher decided to create a fictional company he dubbed "Bat Cave." The prank was fairly well thought out. Bat Cave contacts included Batman, Robin, and even Alfred, the comic book hero's butler. There were detailed entries for the brand of computers used and how many units were installed. He even went to the trouble of identifying some planned activity for the site.

Salespeople at this marketing information firm routinely physically inspected printouts of customer's orders prior to shipping them to the customer. Despite this quality control exercise, the jokester's prank slipped by and shipped out. The first anyone learned of it was from a disgruntled customer. He'd spotted the obviously made-up site and contacts and called, very upset, demanding to know if the rest of the file was of similar low quality! It took the company a long time to restore that individual's confidence in their product.

Most of the time, there's nothing sinister in the extra or missing information in your file. It's just that not all information is important to all the sources from which you are drawing your records. For instance, a customer record resulting from the return of a warranty card may have accurate company name and address information, but have nothing about the name of the person you need to contact there. This is something you should care about. How often do you open mail addressed to your job title without your name? People generally toss this generic mail in the trash. Other missing data may include phone numbers, job responsibilities, industry classification, household size, and many other factors. To come up with the most useful database you can, you're going to have to find a source and a process to ensure the completeness of your data.

Conversion is another opportunity for error in consolidating data. The databases from which you are compiling your central database may have many differing file formats, data headers, record lengths, and so on that make it difficult to accurately translate information from one to the other. Addresses, for instance, may consist of one or more lines for the street address, plus additional lines for the city, state, and postal codes. Some databases may have an entry for the country; others won't. If you blindly import a record with two address lines into a database that anticipates only one line, you may inadvertently be lopping off essential information. Again, this is a problem best dealt with by planning in advance. But it's safe to say that even the most conscientious effort to accurately convert data will introduce some errors that have to be dealt with after the fact.

Even Dell Computer, often held as a paragon of direct marketing competence, sometimes faced intractable problems with merging data from two sources. The Dell Order Management System, used to track and control customer orders, created customer numbers in one format. Dell's prospecting system that went by the acronym PROS used another. Furthermore, customer numbers could change in either system. Despite Dell's expertise at both direct marketing and information technology, getting these two databases to synchronize with one another was a constant struggle.

As we've pointed out, the inevitable passage of time and the constant mobility of people and businesses are two major forces that are working against database accuracy. Here's how it works: Some 25 percent to 40 percent of any database file is in flux at any one time. People move, people change jobs, switch titles. People retire, die, or no longer respond to surveys. It happens. About 1 percent of the content of a typical business-to-business database goes out of date each week.

When you're dealing with individual contacts in businesses, the rate of errors may even be higher. One database that specializes in tracking information industry executives reports that 6 percent of the file changes every week. Job titles perhaps change most frequently. An internal study at one of our clients found 14 shifts in 10 months in the title and name of the person at the company who would be the best purchasing contact for a particular set of products. Information changes from week to week. Consumer marketers are a little luckier than the B2B set. One survey indicates that 1 percent of these files change every two weeks.

Good data hygiene starts with building a solid database using the process described in Step 2. After you've built your database, you must verify the data it contains. You can do this by having salespeople or others call to confirm and update information contained in the records. You can automate the task by comparing your data with verified data in other databases. For instance, the National Change of Address (NCOA) Database consists of information on businesses that have filed permanent changes of address with the U.S. Postal Service. Basic data hygiene requires you to check your list against the NCOA file. This can be done through service bureaus.

Data assessment and verification is a job that has to be done—done well and done consistently. If you want your marketing messages to reach the right people, data integrity and accuracy requires commitment to an ongoing effort.

None of this is particularly easy or fun. Automating the task using service bureaus may be prohibitively costly for small companies. Verifying even small databases manually, on the other hand, can consume considerable amounts of time that might be dedicated to other more productive endeavors.

Analyzing Your Data

Analyzing your data is where you get down to the nitty-gritty of asking: Can it answer the questions I need answered? If you have gathered the right information, the answer will consistently be yes. Analyzing marketing information uses powerful and flexible tools for data mining and modeling to get maximum value out of the information you have gathered—sometimes creating new information in the process.

Before we go into analyzing data, understand that, while it may seem almost magical in its ability to extract meaning from numbers, analysis has its limits. For one thing, you usually look at marketing data in terms of categories such as high-income households, customers, Northeastern manufacturing firms, companies with more than 400 employees, and so on. When you lump customers and prospects into categories, you necessarily lose some detail and data. For instance, if your analysis categorizes households into those with incomes of more than $50,000 and those with incomes of less than $50,000, you're assuming a household with $51,000 in income will act similarly to one with $510,000. Understanding that analysis has limits will help you know what do with the results of your analysis and to design refined approaches that can provide more useful answers.

Data Mining

Data mining is the technique of distilling information from large quantities of data by identifying and analyzing trends and relationships.

You'll hear data mining referred to in fields from medical research to preventing fraud in financial services. In marketing, the idea is to examine customer and prospect information in your marketing database for the purpose of identifying ways to leverage customers to extract maximum value. Here are some of the ways data mining is used with marketing databases:

- Predict customer buying behavior.
- Direct marketing to prospects most likely to respond.
- Identify your most profitable customers.
- Optimize your wallet share.
- Identify and profile customers most likely to defect.
- Measure the effectiveness of specific advertising campaigns.
- Cross-sell to customers based on past product purchases.

One good example of the value of data mining is in analyzing Web site traffic logs. These logs can quickly grow to enormous size on a heavily trafficked site. They can contain all sorts of valuable information, such as:

- Where a visitor came from before visiting your site.
- Which pages he or she viewed.
- How long they spent on each page.
- In what order they viewed pages.
- What was the last page they saw before leaving.
- The busiest times of day for the site.

Data mining involves analyzing the raw statistical records in your Web traffic log to isolate these useful pieces of information. The analysis can be very helpful not only in designing a Web site but in helping you to understand your customers and prospects and how to sell to them better. For instance, a page that many visit just before leaving the site may have a problem such as a marketing message that turns your customers and prospects off and sends them searching elsewhere to make a purchase.

Modeling

Modeling is the process of using your information about purchase histories to predict the type of customer or prospect who is most likely to engage in the desired behavior.

Being able to focus your efforts on those people most likely to yield results is clearly a big help in crafting a cost-effective marketing initiative. Modeled data provides enhanced flexibility in your marketing programs. Like turning up or down the volume control on your car radio, modeling allows you to dial into your marketing database to better address your short-term and long-term business issues and opportunities.

Modeled data is usually scored and stored so you can select it in prioritized fashion according to whatever attributes or criteria you included in the model. Using a model to predict behaviors of groups of customers and prospects, you can identify specific segments to include in your marketing efforts by specifying the number of names you want or by requesting a certain score, representing the likelihood that the target will respond in the desired way. To get maximum value from your marketing database, you will almost certainly want to apply modeling tools to it.

Modeling uses a suite of statistical tools, including regression analysis, to extract information from databases. Multiple regression analysis, a standby of direct marketers, is used when you are dealing with a situation where more than one variable is likely to affect the desired outcome. For instance, multiple regression analysis can help you analyze a set of data to find out whether customers who are (1) single, (2) heads of household, and (3) residing in a given ZIP code are more likely to exhibit the desired behavior than married men living elsewhere.

Sounds simple, but we advise caution. When you have numerous variables interacting in a modeling exercise, it's quite possible to have an unimportant variable impact the creation of the model. If you did a statistical analysis of companies buying from your firm, you might find that they were based in the western United States and had annual revenues of over $10 million. You could use this analysis to create a profile of likely prospects. The problem with this is that we know that not all companies in the western United States have revenues over $10 million, and vice versa. If we create a model that has a western location and plus-$10 million sales as independent variables, we're going to get many companies that are not actually likely candidates.

In this case, you can improve the analysis by adding a third variable, such as one for companies that are both western and over $10 million in sales. But it takes knowledge of business, and of markets, as well as a smattering of understanding about statistics, to be able to evaluate and improve on the results of modeling.

When you're sitting down to study a new topic, whether it's an upgraded version of the software you use most, or how to sell a new product to a new market, it pays to first assess what information you have about the topic, then examine that information to see what it can tell you. Then, and only then, are you ready to learn how to leverage your customers to extract maximum value.

Facts to Remember

- When you put in bad data and do nothing to change it, you get out bad data. In DIGS, the most critical variable in determining the success of any marketing effort is not the cleverness of the copy or the power of the offer. The most important attribute of a successful campaign is the quality of your marketing data.
- Which missing data is important? There is only one answer to this question: The data you need to answer the questions you are asking of the database.
- Data assessment and verification is a job that has to be done—done well and done consistently. If you want your marketing messages to reach the right people, data integrity and accuracy requires commitment to an ongoing effort.
- Analyzing your data is where you get down to the nitty-gritty of asking: Can the data answer the questions I need answered? If you have gathered the right information, the answer will consistently be yes. Analyzing marketing information uses powerful and flexible tools for data mining and modeling to get maximum value out of the

information you have gathered—sometimes creating new information in the process.

- Data mining is the technique of distilling information from large quantities of data by identifying and analyzing trends and relationships.
- Modeling is the process of using your information about purchase histories to predict the type of customer or prospect who is most likely to engage in the desired behavior.

STEP

4

Placing People in Value Segments

Computer users know Dell Computer for selling good computers at reasonable prices and for its outstanding customer service. But to observers of the general business scene, Dell is known more for its business model than for its products, pricing, or service. Build-to-order is the foundation of the Dell business model, the basis from which all its competitive advantages spring. Assembling computers to individual specifications as orders come in allows the company to maintain very little inventory, order parts only when they are required to build an order (often after the customer has already paid for the system), and offer the freshest technology available in the marketplace. Because it has always dealt directly with its customers, Dell knows its customers and their needs much more fully than other computer companies. And being able to put new technology—higher margin technology—into users' hands more quickly than its competitors gives Dell a privileged position

Figure 4.1 Business Model

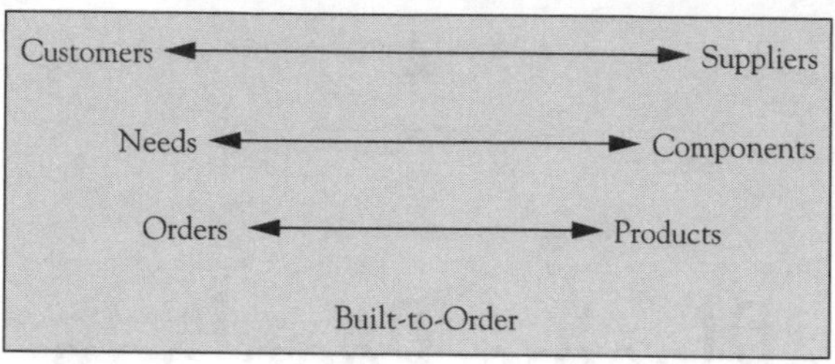

when dealing with suppliers as well. Figure 4.1 shows one view of the fundamentals of the Dell direct business model.

Analysis of customer orders provides Dell with specific insight about what types of computers and what specific configurations are going to be popular in the marketplace. Understanding the customers' buying patterns also provides valuable input that is factored into Dell's pricing strategies, product announcements, and service offerings. These are some of the basics of the build-to-order, direct model that has powered Dell's astounding growth.

The build-to-order model is more than a tool for managing inventory, supplier relationships, and customer behavior. As Dell Computer developed more sophisticated and indepth intelligence about their customers and prospects, they began to develop specific marketing strategies to extract additional business from their current clients and new programs to attract high value prospects. Because they could triangulate information from multiple data points, they were able to assign customers a specific ranking based on the value they provided to the company. This approach of *Value Segmentation* is at the heart of this book.

Value Segmentation is the practice of using the combination of definitive analytical numbers and subjective opinions and insights to generate an assessment of overall customer value to your organization.

Many successful companies have a history of doing this, especially the larger catalog companies. But Value Segmentation is not only for the Land's Ends and Sharper Images of the world. Value Segmentation is similar in concept to some other marketing tools that businesses of all sizes are already familiar with—Lifetime Value and Lifestyle Segmentation. Lifetime Value (LTV), for example, is a way to evaluate a customer's importance to you. A basic calculation of LTV multiplies a customer's average annual expenditures times the number of years that customer can be expected to remain a loyal customer. A more complicated LTV computation by, for instance, a financial institution might consider how much income a customer was providing in the form of insufficient funds fees, monthly service charges, interest received on loans, and special services such as traveler's checks. To determine LTV, they might use a retention rate. LTV may also take into consideration the costs to service an account. That same financial services company must pay close attention to cost of capital involved in servicing its customers, basing its calculations on customers' net present value.

Value Segmentation is data driven and goes beyond LTV by helping you guide your marketing efforts and manage your business. LTV could be described as offering a backward perspective, while Value Segmentation focuses forward. Unlike the typical LTV analysis, that looks at how much a customer is spending with you now, Value Segmentation looks at how much a customer is spending in total for products and services that are similar to yours. Although it includes quantitative information, Value Segmentation's qualitative input makes it equally an academic exercise and application of street smarts. It takes into consideration relationships established within the account as well as product plans and market changes within your industry. The distinction between Value Segmentation and LTV is especially important when, as is usually the case, you don't have as many data points about your customers and prospects as you would like. Value Segmentation, because of its qualitative features, can still provide insight and direction to your sales and marketing efforts.

Lifestyle Segmentation describes the practice of categorizing consumers based on their preferences, activities, beliefs, and other psychographic data. While Lifestyle Segmentation can be incorporated into your Value Segmentation methodology, it is important to understand that it is not the same thing. In Value Segmentation, lifestyles are important in understanding if a customer can be motivated to become a better customer. The traditional marketer uses lifestyle information to develop a creative message or to select people from a database. An example is: You are a golf club manufacturer. In traditional marketing, a company may choose golf enthusiasts for a mailing. They may incorporate golf visuals throughout or perhaps some golf swing education. In Value Segmentation, we take it a step further and want to know how much the golf enthusiast spends on equipment. If he is a weekend hacker playing par-3 courses, he may not be right for your company. But if he plays 18 holes at a private club three times a week, he is much more appealing. Both players may describe themselves the same, but one is much more valuable than the other.

At its core, Value Segmentation is set on two axes (Figure 4.2). On the vertical axis, Value Segmentation plots your target customers' or prospects' overall available budget—the money they have to spend on product and services that you sell. Whether you are selling semiconductors or soda pop, your customers typically have a fixed sum of money they can spend.

On the horizontal axis, Value Segmentation charts what percentage of this budget you are capturing. We call this your firm's share of their wallet or wallet share. The more you sell to this customer, the higher your percentage of their overall budget becomes. This book is about maximizing that percentage. This is the Relationship Continuum because a business relationship is about sales.

The power of the Value Segment Matrix is that every person within your organization can understand the concept and is often able to instinctively assign specific customers to specific quadrants within this nine-box grid. The simplicity of this matrix can be a galvanizing communications device and something that we will

Figure 4.2 Value Segmentation Matrix

	Conquest	Grow	Own
	Relationship Continuum		
Available Budget — High	$$$	$$$$	$$$$$
Available Budget — Medium	$$	$$$	$$$$
Available Budget — Low	$	$$	$$$
	Low	Medium	High
		Wallet Share	

speak about more in Step 6 when we talk about Organizational Magnification.

Do not underestimate the power of the Value Segmentation grid. Plotting customers to their position within this matrix often reveals some disturbing discoveries. Surprisingly, when companies go through this exercise they tend to find that their actual wallet share is often less than what they thought it was within their larger or strategic accounts. Patrick's own experience points out how costly overestimating your position within an account can be.

When Patrick was a sales executive with a marketing intelligence company, he landed a $1 million deal that was, at the time, an unprecedentedly large sale for his employer. In fact, the arrangement set a new pricing threshold for his industry. Given the circumstances, he was understandably confident that he had extracted maximum value from the account. Then he found out that his huge new account was spending yet another half-million dollars with his largest competitor. While it didn't make his sale any smaller, the new information did unmistakably mean that he had left a potential half-million dollars in revenues on the table because he failed to understand the true potential value of his account. Rather than getting 100 percent of the client's available budget, he had captured only two-thirds. Its relationship was not as strong as he thought. And remember, a business relationship is about sales. When he found out about his competitor's success, Patrick's boss' backhanded "thanks a million" compliment stung as much as it flattered. An accurate understanding of your position on the Relationship Continuum within your accounts can keep any salesperson from making the mistake of settling for too little.

One of the great benefits of Value Segmentation is that it helps you and your company focus more on your customers and prospects and less on your products (Figure 4.3). If your company is like most, the natural tendency is to attack marketing from a product perspective. Perhaps, a better approach is to understand who your best customers are, what their needs are, and then develop products and services that meet those needs. Value Segmentation, with its foundation on understanding customers, facilitates this kind of an attitude shift and enables you to leverage your relationship with current clients to extract additional business from them. It forces a balanced consideration of what you have to sell and what you need to provide. It's important to keep in mind that this is not an *either-or* equation. It's an *and* equation. It's not how much your customers have already purchased—it's about what and how much they should be buying from you.

Figure 4.3 Market Map

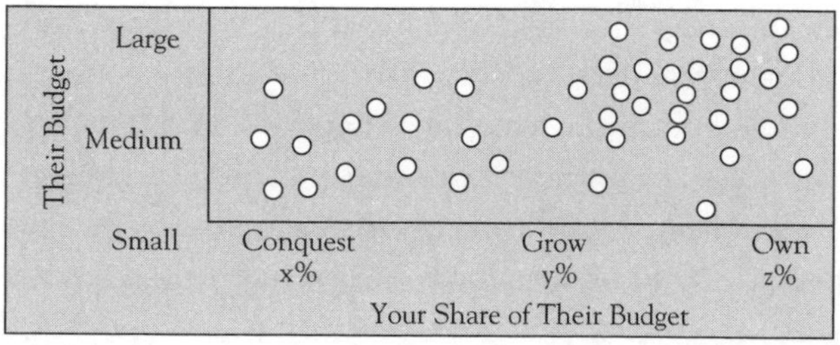

Value Segmentation also provides crisis insurance as well. When things start to go bad—a poor financial quarter, a poor product release, a strong competitor advance—most companies scramble to analyze their accounts. Suddenly, the question "Who can we sell this to?" becomes of paramount importance. Value Segmentation takes the guesswork out of the equation and calms the storm. Smart marketers simply investigate their Value Segmentation Matrix, home in on organizations that can be easily activated, and approach them with an appealing offer. Rather than scrambling to find out information about their customers, these empowered marketers are applying the intelligence they already have to engage a customer in a business opportunity that makes sense to both organizations. This applied learning approach strengthens the relationship you have with these customers and extracts additional business while enhancing customer satisfaction.

For all its power, Value Segmentation is a remarkably flexible tool. A small business can use this simple analytical tool to gain new insights into long-time customers or to evaluate expanding into new markets. You can assign customers to different values in multiple value matrixes depending on factors such as the product you are trying to sell, the industry influence that the target exhibits, or how easy it is for you to gain sponsorship and access to the executive suite. Accounts can have membership in multiple matrixes. You may have several product matrixes, for example. If you are a furniture store, a client may have a higher ranking in the accessories matrix than he has in your wood products because his purchases are primarily lamps and rugs.

This level of scoring can be very useful when you have an end-of-life or excess inventory situation with either of these products. While it is clearly powerful when paired with a business model like Dell's build-to-order model, Value Segmentation is not limited to companies having this model. No matter what your business model is, you can profit by knowing more about your customers, and assigning values to them based on that knowledge.

To get an idea of how Value Segmentation can help refine marketing into a powerful yet highly flexible business tool, consider what we did using seasonality for a Value Segmentation exercise at Dell. Many if not most companies consider seasonal influences such as holidays, fiscal year ends, and back-to-school periods in their planning and marketing. One big seasonal influence that affects just about everyone who sells to the federal government is the buying season that occurs in August, September, and October. This three-month period is powered by the federal government's "use it or lose it" budgeting philosophy.

Considering seasonal influences such as the federal buying season represents an intelligent approach to setting goals and expectations, but it is basic marketing. It doesn't really require an advanced understanding of your customer's behavior and how to influence it. At Dell, we combined seasonality and DIGS-type customer knowledge to create a powerful tool for increasing sales.

To start with, we built a detailed blueprint of our customers' locations and overlaid external information about computer systems they had installed and what they were planning to buy. We purchased this information from external data suppliers who obtained it by interviewing decision makers within government agencies. By combining our own internal information with external data, we developed a location-by-location, product-by-product understanding of each site's individual purchasing power and an estimate of what part of their current available budget was earmarked for the products and services we could provide. We assumed that personal computers had a three-year life cycle, meaning that 33 percent of their installed inventory was up for bid at any one time. If the customer had 100 desktops installed, we estimated that 33 of them were always available for replacement. Using our average selling price for desktops, we calculated what their budget was and what percentage of their overall budget we had captured based on our orders. We also considered the customer's overall installed base. For instance, was he typically purchasing current technology or was he one release back? Did he purchase off the General Services Administration contract or from a Blanket Purchase Agreement (BPA)? We then factored in our relationship with the account. What percentage of their wallet were we getting? Did we have access to the top decision makers? Were they buying all three of our hardware product lines? Factoring in all of these considerations, we assigned our accounts to specific value segments.

What we found sometimes did not please us. Among other things, we found that one department, an agency we thought of as one of our premier accounts because they were buying many desktop computers from us, actually made less than 10 percent of their overall purchases from us. We knew we had competitors in the account, but we had no idea that we were so low on the totem pole. We had treated them like kings, provided them with onsite field service personnel and numerous other "percs." And yet we weren't even getting a meaningful share of their business. Nothing opens your eyes like a cold splash of water!

One of the tenets of Value Segmentation is that in order to accurately segment customers by value, you must understand the drivers of your business—why do people buy from you and how do you sell to them profitability?

To try to understand what was going on at Dell, we looked at the drivers of our business. Using the data we had already accumulated, we investigated specific behavior relating to early adoption of new technology. To do so, we looked at what percentage of a customer's past purchases had occurred at specific points in time—days, weeks, months—after the announcement of new products. We were able to see, for example, that one of our customers transitioned 35 percent of their desktop purchases to our newest technology within three weeks of our product's announcement. Quarter after quarter, product announcement after product announcement, their behavior was consistent. Their performance on this score enabled us to tag them as high on the early adopter characteristic. So guess what we did? We built their appetite directly into our forecast and, by identifying all of the other early adopters within our market, our division consistently outperformed all other Dell divisions on our forecast accuracy. Likewise, we tagged specific accounts that required longer product transitions. We reserved specific product for them, making their transitions to newer technology a smooth process. Their customer satisfaction soared and these accounts became a vital component of our end-of-life (EOL) strategies. By offering these long-transition accounts small discounts early in the EOL process, we were able to get rid of older technology at profitable margins rather than scrambling to get rid of these systems at fire sale prices.

These experiences show how Value Segmentation can incorporate highly refined aspects of customer behavior. Value Segmentation works as sort of sliding scale whereby a single site may have multiple values based on different scenario requirements. The segmentation of our accounts by various value criteria enabled us to devise a sophisticated and sensible plan for maximizing sales to our government clients.

Our success in managing our product line transitions had strong leveraging effects in other areas of our business, too. For example, Intel and Microsoft loved us because we could distribute new product very quickly, since we knew where our early adopters were and could track them location by location and product by product. Also, when other government agencies became authorized to make purchases using another agency's contract, we knew who the decision makers were in every location of those newly authorized agencies and turned on our marketing engine to tell them about what equipment they could buy from us off of that extended contract. The combined result of all these influences was market share gains in affinity agencies, and the establishment of new footholds in additional clients.

These kinds of experiences with Value Segmentation are not unique or even unusual. In fact, this doesn't tell the whole story of the benefits you can expect. If you can predict with accuracy who will buy how much of your new product as well as when they will buy, you can provide manufacturing with very accurate forecasts. Manufacturing in turn is better able to purchase just enough supply of the right components to build the products as the customer ordered them. This was the interlocking beauty of the Dell direct model and shows the interdependencies and intricacies of all of the parts working together in an integrated fashion. Seasonality? In a sense, it is. But it's clearly a far cry from the primitive sense of seasonality employed in conventional marketing, and illustrates neatly just now much better the Direct Impact Growth System is than anything you are likely to be using.

Techniques

Let's say you're sold on trying Value Segmentation. How do you do it? Value Segmentation is basically a process of three steps: *Exploration, Evaluation,* and *Placement.* In the Exploration phase, you are using your Market Development System database of knowledge to create segments and then to profile them. In Evaluation, you are deciding who among your customers and prospects is most valuable to you based on your attributes. Finally, Placement is the process of assigning a value to specific customer segments using the Value Segmentation Matrix reflecting both the phase of your relationship and your share of customer purchases.

Exploration

In Exploration, the first step of Value Segmentation, you are delving into the information you have collected about your customers and prospects with the intent of creating customer segments and profiles.

The idea here is to go beyond the first cut of dividing customers based on their purchases from you. While purchasing is the focus of your marketing effort, you may very well find it useful to be able to categorize your customers by using demographic, geographic, or industry specific information.

Use your Market Development System database to create profiles for each customer segment. Take care to slice your customers into usable segments, not general markets. What does this mean? A market might be defined as "small business owners." That's too general to be of use. It will include people who you are unlikely to ever sell to and who, in any event, you can't define well enough to devise an intelligent offer or communications plan.

A segment, for our purposes, describes a group of customers or prospects that have similar attitudes toward you and your company. A different profile, therefore, will be composed of customers who have different attitudes from that first group. The reason attitudes are important is that your customers' attitudes toward you drive the way you market to them. For example, one important attitude trait is willingness to buy from you. This can be figured by looking at purchases from you in the past, or by purchases from similar providers, as well as information such as survey data in which prospects express a willingness to buy from you. To identify and track customers who exhibit similar attitudes, you will use various characteristics such as age, company size, ZIP code, and so on.

You can, in theory and sometimes in practice, boil your profiles down to the individual customer because, strictly speaking, nobody has precisely the same attitude toward you as anybody else. Some markets are small enough to easily segment by individual customers. If you are a business-to-business marketer selling to just a few specialized companies, you can individually track the key people in each company or location, plus whatever other companies you identify as prospects. Customers and prospects like these may well be important enough to your business to justify individual marketing approaches and true one-to-one personal relationships.

Such a level of detail is impractical, however, unless your market is very small. For companies addressing larger markets, the question arises as to how small should the segments be? There is no single answer to this. Dell's broadest set of profiles recognizes approximately a dozen classes of customers, including health care, federal government, state and local government, education, consumer, and business customers divided into small business, three varieties of corporate customers based on number of employees, global or multinational customers, and a separate category for Internet service providers, who have special interest in Dell's high-end server products.

There is no one answer. Assuming that your market is large enough to have more than a handful of customers and prospects, practicality and cost issues should help define the appropriate segment strategy for you. When customers in a segment differ very little in their attitude toward you, or when you don't have enough data points to distinguish between segments or, perhaps, the computing horsepower to manage more, you can cut your segments off at that point. Be aware of the risk of analysis paralysis in making these decisions. More important than identifying the best answer is to identify a good answer and then get started implementing it. If you embrace the idea of learning along the way, begin executing your plan and document your findings. You will be able to tweak and improve it to get closer to the theoretical ideal.

The idea with segments is to tag these target groups using the specific attributes of each group. Tags commonly used in consumer marketing include gender, age, locale, household size, and household income. Like Dell, marketers segment business customers based on company size, number of employees, location, industry, and other attributes.

We've already said that no database has everything a savvy marketer would want to know about a market, but it's not enough to accept that limitation. You have to know as precisely as possible just where your database lives up to its potential and where it falls down. To assess database elements, consider the two types of attributes for your customers and prospects shown in Figure 4.4.

Figure 4.4 Attributes

Consumer:	Business:
• Zip code	• SIC code
• Household income	• Zip code
• Household assets	• Number of employees
• Own/rent home	• Annual sales
• Education level	• Profits
• Ages of family members	• Assets
• Credit record	• Fiscal year
• Date customer acquired	• Principal officers
• Date of most recent purchase (recency)	• Subsidiary locations
• Frequency of purchases (frequency)	• Installed base
• Dollar value of purchases (monetary)	• Date customer acquired
• Number of annual purchases	• Date of most recent purchase (recency)
• Source of original lead	• Frequency of purchases (frequency)
• Promotional history	• Dollar value of purchases (monetary)
	• Number of annual purchases
	• Source of original lead
	• Promotional history

Hard Attributes

The first one of these is the hard attributes. These can include company size, SIC code, and other elements for business-to-business marketers. Consumer marketers have hard attributes for location, family size, household assets, and many other traits. You can obtain hard attributes from your own internal databases, including sales transaction records, as well as third-party external sources. Hard attributes can be gathered from surveys, U.S. Census polls, and other sources in addition to your data.

Soft Attributes

Soft attributes are different and include the budget process—a key attribute in profiling government agencies as compared to corporate customers. The buying or decision-making process followed by a customer or prospect is another soft attribute. This attribute might indicate that buying decisions at this group of companies are made at the local level as opposed to all buying decisions coming through a central office.

Where are you going to get this soft information? The first place you should look is internally—to your salesforce. Salespeople know or soon learn about the budget cycles and buying processes of their customers. Unfortunately, this information is rarely documented. It exists in their heads and you may have to wrestle it out of them.

Some salespeople may not want to give you this information. To allay their fears, you must show them the power of Value Segmentation within their territory. Offer to do a territory analysis for them and then sit down and personally share it with them. Engaging naysayers directly often makes them advocates. Once they accept the process, they'll usually agree to provide the data and be accountable for the completeness of their territory's data.

Focus groups represent another source of soft data. These are informal collections of 10 or so people who are brought together for the purposes of obtaining their views on specific products, companies, needs, and other marketing concerns. Focus groups can provide useful soft information such as how people will react to a product name or direct marketing letter you are considering. To be useful, focus groups have to be led by a skilled moderator experienced at drawing out useful information. The participants also have to be selected carefully from your customers and prospects to make sure they reflect a representative sample of your marketplace.

The goal of gathering all these attributes and using them to create profiles is to improve your understanding of customers and prospects. To successfully craft an effective marketing system and leverage the Direct Impact Growth System, you have to know who you sell to, what is important to them, and how they can be sold. The drivers of their buying behavior may be complex and unpredictable, so it can take large arrays of relevant data to grasp their motivations. It bears repeating that the goal here is not to know everything about your customers, but to know enough to get started and learn as you go. Our advice is: Document what you already know, take steps to learn more, and get started so you can begin to extract additional value from your customers and prospects.

Evaluation

The second step, Evaluation, is about using your profiles to decide who among your customers and prospects is most valuable to you. You examine purchase history data and compare it to the profiles you have created in order to be able to predict likely purchasers or growth clients.

When dealing with large numbers of people and businesses, big company marketers use statistical tools to select and analyze samples so that they don't have to examine every single customer, prospect, and transaction. Statistics is a technical field and is also, by its nature, an inexact science, being based on estimates, samples, and probabilities. For these reasons, you will probably use trained statisticians to analyze your data and assign levels of confidence to the conclusions drawn from it.

This is how the technique can work: You are selling construction project management software and you want to determine who your best customers are, with the idea of using this information to tag customers and prospects and create profiles of unusually good customers. Using the sales transaction information in your database, rank order your customers and identify the 10 percent of whom have bought the most from you in the past year. By ranking customers according to various attributes, you happen to discover that your best customers are highway construction companies. Using this knowledge, logic leads you to select similar customers and prospects that are transportation engineers as an affinity group that is likely to be a good group of customers as well.

You will use other tags to similarly identify better, good, and poor customers and prospects, and determine similarities among these customer groups. Your ultimate goal of the exploration step is to identify a prioritized list of targets for your marketing efforts. What if you don't have the resources to retain the services of statisticians to analyze your data? When dealing with smaller universes of customers and prospects, you can get a good feel for your market by simply looking it over. Scanning a subset of your database—say a few hundred or a thousand accounts—will quickly give you a good grasp of the nature of its contents. In many cases, you may find that looking at market information confirms information you already understood intuitively. For instance, you can reassure yourself that, indeed, your best customers are midsize firms, or that you are weak on the East Coast. This doesn't require profound analysis and, coupled with good street smarts, can make any database a muscular marketing tool for companies of any size.

Placement

The third step, Placement, plots your customers into your Value Segmentation Matrix.

Despite its essential simplicity, by now it is probably clear that the Value Segmentation Matrix (Figure 4.5) requires a diligent effort to gather and understand information about your customers and prospects, their relationships with you and how they fit into your corporate objectives.

It's also true that the messages the Value Segmentation Matrix carries are often complex. For example, a first cut at understanding and employing this nine-box matrix in direct marketing might involve ending or drastically curtailing your efforts at marketing to the customers and prospects inhabiting the box on the bottom row of the left column. These customers and prospects have little to

Figure 4.5 Value Segmentation Matrix

		Conquest	Grow	Own
		Relationship Continuum		
Available Budget	High	$$$	$$$$	$$$$$
	Medium	$$	$$$	$$$$
	Low	$	$$	$$$
		Low	Medium	High
		Wallet Share		

spend and little loyalty to your company. You could probably expend your resources with larger effect elsewhere.

But the Value Segmentation Matrix is a dynamic entity just like the markets it portrays. You need to understand the contents of this low-Value, low-Relationships box even if you don't intend to focus marketing efforts on it. For instance, you can profitably compare information about this box's current contents to its contents on previous occasions. Are there more companies in it than before? Is their average potential value to you higher or lower than it was? Changes in these amounts can suggest new trends in the marketplace as well as the marketplace's perception of you. You may also wish to employ this box when pursuing specialized goals. For instance, you could use this box to help reach end-of-quarter revenue goals, but leave it out of your long-term relationship efforts. In many other ways, segmenting your market using your Value Segmentation Matrix can provide powerful yet easy-to-grasp tools for managing your business using the Direct Impact Growth System.

By being able to categorize customers based on available budget and your wallet share, you can select one or more boxes in the matrix on which to focus your marketing efforts. You will be guided in this effort by the corporate objectives you have drafted. You can craft individual messages and offers for each box. Should you wish, you can average the Relationship and Value factors for all companies in each box and treat them more or less the same, in terms of how you market to them. Or you can slice each box into additional segments, and approach each in a different way.

Using the Value Segmentation Matrix

The horizontal axis of the Value Segmentation Matrix replicates the Relationship Continuum, charting the development of your relationship with a customer as you move from first acquaintance through increasing familiarity and acceptance to a final stage where you are the customer's default choice. It helps you track and compare quantities such as your perceived relationship with customers—what you feel about the customer—with the received relationship—what you're actually receiving in the form of orders.

The key concept here is the share of purchase or share of wallet you have with each customer. This is expressed as the percentage of your customer's total budget for buying offerings like those you sell that is actually going for your products and services. If a given customer spends $1,000 a year on products and services like yours, and your sales to that customer are $100 a year, then you have a 10 percent share of wallet. Share of wallet is a good measure of the relationship you have developed with a customer.

While it's easy to find out how much you sell to a given customer or group of customers, finding out customer budgets can be trickier. Customers and prospects may be reluctant to provide information about their purchasing power to vendors. This is where third-party market research can come in handy. Companies providing industry-specific market research employ batteries of trained and diligent interviewers, as well as many inexpensive and effective tools such as online surveys, that can gather surprising amounts of information about purchasing plans. Obtaining this information and matching it to your sales figures provides you with the share of wallet information you need to fill out the Relationship Continuum (Figure 4.6) and the Value Segmentation Matrix.

Stage One: Conquest, you are just beginning your relationship with a customer. In the Conquest stage, the customer is buying little or nothing from you and may not even be aware of you. Customers at the Conquest stage represent the most challenging in terms of creating awareness of and preference for your company, but they also have the highest potential for improvement because they begin at such a low base. Depending on how well populated the squares at the later two states of your Value Segmentation Matrix are, you may choose to concentrate your efforts on these Conquest-stage customers and prospects, trying to turn them into later-stage customers, or you may divert resources away from the Conquest column to focus on people who are already partially in your camp.

Stage Two: Grow the Relationship is the stage during which you are increasing the amount of their available budget—share of wallet—that you are getting. At this point, the customer has selected you as an acceptable supplier but hasn't yet decided you are the *best* provider. You therefore have tremendous upside potential and should work diligently to extract all the value you can from these

Figure 4.6 Relationship Continuum

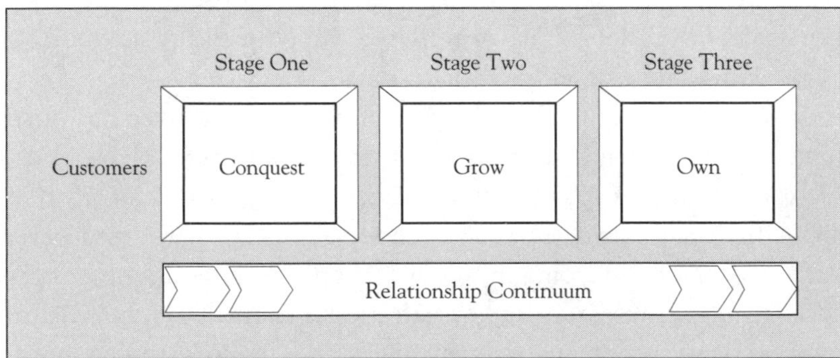

accounts. Bear in mind, however, that just because you are in the door doesn't mean that you will be able to capture all of their business. Some firms restrict the percent of their purchases that go to a given supplier. You may have to weight your estimation of the account's potential using what you know about your customer's buying restrictions.

At Dell, we had many customers residing in the final *Stage Three: Earned Loyalty*. For them, Dell was the first choice for any product that they used and we sold. This is obviously a desirable state for a company; few sellers would complain about being considered as the default solution for their customers. Not all your customers, nor any company's customers, will always be in Stage Three: Earned Loyalty. Customers are continually becoming dissatisfied, changing their needs or otherwise finding reasons to leave the fold. They may retreat to an earlier, less committed stage, or leave you altogether in favor of another vendor. If you know erosion is happening, you can take active steps to counter it. If you do not, you may find that all of your customers have left you and your business has evaporated without knowing why.

Customer churn is going to happen so you must shore up the banks of your current accounts while prospecting for new customers. New prospects are continually entering on the lefthand side of the Relationship Continuum and beginning to make their way across the levels of familiarity with and commitment to your company and its offerings. Tracking the number and placement of new customers, and doing what you can to influence their behavior is also essential to maintaining a vibrant market for your products and services.

It's natural and appropriate to place most of your marketing emphasis on extracting maximum value from your existing customers. These are the people most likely to engage in the desired behavior you are looking for because, among other reasons, they know you and you know them. Managing prospects rarely results in as rapid or as satisfying a result as leveraging customer relationships. But it's a mistake to ignore the prospect side of the Market Management

System. If you don't replenish your customer base, you will find yourself devoting more and more attention to a smaller and smaller group of customers. Many companies have fallen into this trap and, one unhappy day, suddenly realize they are in a serious fix, often without sufficient time or the appropriate resources to repair it.

You may be able to make Prospect Relationship Management (PRM) more palatable if you look at it in the way you might view an invitation to two cocktail parties. One gathering is being hosted by an old friend and is certain to feature many other long-time colleagues. You'll be comfortable there, undoubtedly. The other event is sponsored by a recent acquaintance. If you go to this bash, odds are good you won't know many or even anyone else there. The benefit of attending the second party, however, is that you will meet new people and expand your circle of friends. If you go only to old friends' parties—or market to tried-and-true customers—you will be comfortable, contented—and courting eventual disaster.

Value Axis

The Value Axis of the Value Segmentation Matrix relates to your customers' budgets for purchasing products and services like yours in a different way from the Relationship Continuum. Instead of assessing them and ranking them based on the percentage of their budgets that you are capturing, it looks at their total budgets.

Customer budgets are important because customers' budgets more or less equals their potential value to you. The higher the potential value, the greater your effort should be to capture it—all things being equal. However, a customer who spends $10,000 on products like yours in a year is going to be ranked higher than one that spends only $100, even if you're getting all that hundred-dollar customer's business right now. There are limitations to segmenting customers by their budgets. Assigning desirability based on the size of their budget is useful, but doesn't take into consideration all possible variables. For instance, some customers and prospects with large budgets may not be particularly desirable targets for you. They may be overly price sensitive or located in areas you can't cost-effectively serve or support.

Some customers are less efficient profit-producers than others because they require a great deal of after-sale support. Depending on your corporate objectives, you may wish to deemphasis higher revenue, less-efficient customers in favor of small, but more profitable opportunities. That's why you may want to have different axes for your Value Segmentation Matrix. No matter what you're counting, when you start from this beginning point and rank customers by budget or other characteristics, you can define targets appropriate for your corporate initiatives and available marketing resources.

The Value Segmentation Matrix

We once had a music teacher who described his process of learning about composing as follows: "When you first start composing, the big question is: Which note should I play now? So you study scales, chords, melodies, harmonies, and the rest of music theory. You learn that, under the right circumstances, any note will fit anywhere. So after all that, the question is: Which note should I play now?" Marketing is like that; no matter how much you learn about marketing, you're not going to get an answer to the question of what you should do. You'll only learn about the strengths and weaknesses of available options and gain practice with tools for helping you select from among them. Deciding what note to play next is a matter of listening to the music in your head. Deciding how to use Value Segmentation is a matter of paying attention to the corporate objectives you have set.

A question of critical importance is where in the Value Segmentation Matrix you are to expend your energy. You decide which of the nine boxes in the Value Segmentation Matrix will be the focus of your efforts. Should you focus on customers in the box at the bottom on the far left? On those in the top rightmost sector? On both? Your decision will depend on your corporate objectives and market conditions as well as your assessment of the traits of the occupants of the boxes.

There are scores of possible marketing strategies based on selecting any one or any combination of up to eight of the nine boxes to receive the focus of your efforts. Why not go equally after all nine? Napoleon said it best: "He who seeks to be strong everywhere will be strong nowhere." The essence of strategy is focusing your efforts where you believe they will do the most good, not diffusing them equally across every option.

You can also slice any or all of the nine boxes into smaller segments, multiplying your choices. For instance, take the box on the upper right, representing the large-budget customers with whom you have the largest share of wallet. If you want to attack this segment but it is too large or too diverse for you to come up with a suitable one-size-fits-all message and offer, you can divide it other ways. You can overlay SIC codes and cut it up by industry. You can divide it by employee size, geographic location, budget cycle, price sensitivity, or any other attribute you can obtain information on and use in your marketing. For each of these Value Segments, you can devise a separate strategy including offer, message, and contact plan. When amplified in this manner, the simple-looking Value Segmentation Matrix can be the foundation of an extremely complex sophisticated marketing plan.

The first cut many marketers make is to focus on a subset of the nine boxes. One option, for instance, is to focus on the customers with the largest budgets for your product or service (Figure 4.7). Because they have the most to spend, they are probably among your best prospects for generating future growth. These are the customers and prospects in the three boxes along the top. Your initial goal may be to just get your foot in the door and build awareness of your products among the target group. Your strategy for achieving that may start with obtaining soft data about customer preferences that would explain why you are not selling more to these large potential accounts, and then crafting a marketing effort that addresses the issues uncovered.

Another choice might be aimed at your most loyal customers, in the boxes clustered along the righthand side the matrix (Figure 4.8). These are currently buying the largest volume, relative to their overall budgets, from you. You need to know who these people are for defensive reasons if nothing else. If a competitor begins to make inroads to these valued customers, you will want to know about it as soon as possible and take steps to counter the defections. You may want to craft high-level service offerings to keep your top customers from being lured away by competitors. Strategies for reaching these customers may also involve snaring even larger parts of their budgets for the same products and services you are already selling to them. Or, if you are already achieving the maximum practical sales level for existing products, you may be better off devising new products and services to offer these faithful supporters.

Some marketers find the most fertile ground lies somewhere in the middle—the three squares along each axis that represent those who are about average in the size of their budgets and in the share of wallet devoted to you. These middle-of-the-road customers and prospects are often on the edge, ready to become more valuable customers to you with the application of some marketing efforts intelligently directed by the Direct Impact Growth System. Also, because they are average, they may be receiving only average attention from your competitors. Adjusting the amount of attention you pay to an above-average level may turn these average customers into some of

Figure 4.7 Market Map

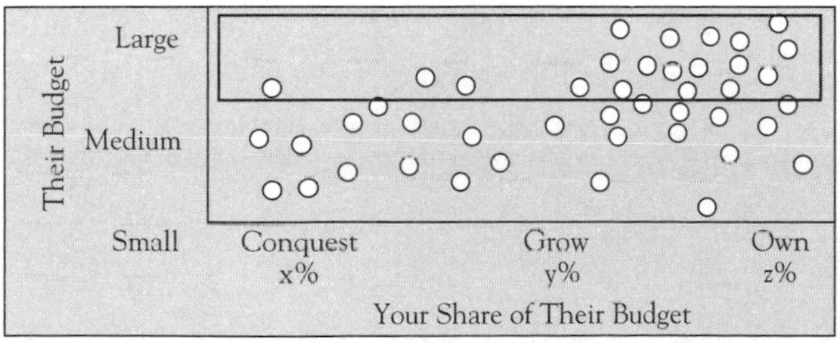

Figure 4.8 Market Map

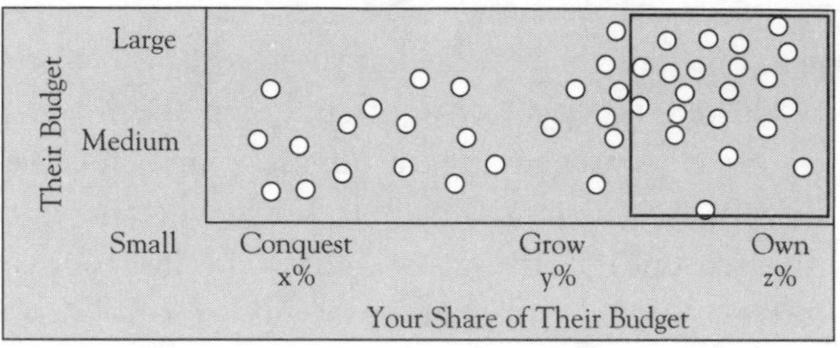

your best accounts. This is still another way in which DIGS can alert you to opportunities to increase your market share.

Summary

After seeing some of the ways in which Value Segmentation can be used, including the kind of work we did with it at Dell, you may be sold on its potential value to you as a marketer, but wondering whether you can afford the time, resources, and desire to Dell-style in-depth Value Segmentation. One answer to that question is another question: Can you afford not to? While we believe we know Value Segmentation as well as any marketers, there's no question that these ideas are out there. If your competitors haven't started similar programs, there's nothing that will keep them from doing so, and doing so before you unless you move with energy.

Also consider that the cost may not be as significant as you expect. Chances are good, for instance, that many companies can apply current efforts at Customer Data Integration to building a customer database suitable for Value Segmentation. And if you don't have a CDI project and aren't concerned enough about competition to dive in headfirst, you can start small and still derive significant benefit from a much simpler Value Segmentation exercise. For instance, you can divide your customers as high, medium, and low in value, based on a smaller set of data such as company sales.

Should you wish to evolve your Value Segmentation further, you can incorporate more specific and sophisticated information including Lifetime Value. The way you use Value Segmentation can change significantly as you obtain more data and more understanding.

Don't wait until you have a perfect database to start using Value Segmentation. Your Value Segmentation Matrix doesn't have to be perfect before it starts helping you grow. As you do more with it, you'll learn more about your customers and the Direct Impact Growth System, and be ready to grow more.

Facts to Remember

- Value Segmentation is the practice of using the combination of definitive analytical numbers and subjective opinions and insights to generate an assessment of overall customer value to your organization.
- One of the tenets of Value Segmentation is that in order to accurately segment customers by value, you must understand the drivers of your business: Why do people buy from you and how do you sell to them profitability?
- Value Segmentation is basically a process of three steps: Exploration, Evaluation, and Placement.
- In Exploration, the first step of Value Segmentation, you are delving into the information you have collected about your customers and prospects with the intent of creating customer segments and profiles.
- The second step, Evaluation, is about using your profiles to decide who among your customers and prospects is most valuable to you. You examine data about purchase history and compare it to the profiles you have created to predict likely purchasers or growth clients.

(Continued)

- The third step, Placement, plots your customers into a two-dimensional space called the Nine-Box Matrix that has as its horizontal axis your Relationship with your customers and, as its vertical axis, their Value to you.
- The horizontal axis of the Value Segmentation Matrix replicates the Relationship Continuum, charting the development of your relationship with a customer as you move from first acquaintance through increasing familiarity and acceptance to a final stage where you are the customer's default choice. It helps you track and compare such quantities as your perceived relationship with customers—what you feel about the customer—with the received relationship—what you're actually receiving in the form of orders.
- The Value Axis of the Value Segmentation Matrix relates to your customers' budgets for purchasing products and services like yours in a different way from the Relationship Continuum. Instead of assessing them and ranking them based on the percentage of their budgets that you are capturing, it looks at their total budgets.
- You decide which of the nine boxes in the Value Segmentation Matrix will be the focus your efforts. Should you focus on customers in the box at the bottom on the far left? On those in the top right sector? On both? Your decision will depend on your corporate objectives and market conditions as well as your assessment of the traits of the occupants of the boxes.
- You don't have to and shouldn't wait until you have a perfect database to start using Value Segmentation. Your Value Segmentation Matrix doesn't have to be flawless before it starts helping you to grow. As you do more with it, you'll learn more about your customers and the Direct Impact Growth System, and be ready to grow more.

PART II

IMPLEMENTATION AND EXECUTION

STEP

5

Planning to Capture Value

If you've ever painted anything such as a house or wall, you know that the activities of planning ahead and preparing the surface to be painted are both time consuming and time rewarding. In the same way, planning your implementation of the Direct Impact Growth System (DIGS), through the use of pro formas, Contact Plans, and other tools of the direct marketer, requires some investment of upfront money and time but will pay off handsomely down the road.

Planning is almost universally practiced in business but still has a somewhat mixed image. On the one hand, you have many corporate managers demanding and requiring annual and quarterly plans for marketing, sales, and other activities from all their reports. Similarly, investors and lenders require business plans to show what use will be made of the money they are making available for investment.

On the other hand, you also have luminaries such as John Sperling, the billionaire entrepreneurial founder, chairman, and

CEO of the University of Phoenix, saying, "Strategic planning is a process and the greatest benefit to be derived from the process is the impact which planning has on the people who do the planning. The plan itself is of secondary importance."

What's the point of planning, as we're recommending in this chapter? Sperling's point is that the process of information-gathering, what-if analysis, and contingency preparation involved in planning is a valuable exercise in and of itself. This is an important point. The by-product of a careful, comprehensive planning effort is a better understanding of your objectives, your marketplace, and how you plan to attack both.

Are there possible risks to planning? Sure there are. Plans require assumptions and assumptions require data to be accurate.

Your plan will evolve over time. It will mature in response to new information gathered, changes in the marketplace, and course corrections in your corporate objectives. Plans are not static. They are directional in nature and always should be. The only thing that should ever be cast in stone is the Ten Commandments and even that took two rounds to make it permanent. To quote Sperling again, this time on the risk of taking plans too literally: "Strategic plans are direction signs, not road maps. Both internal and external environments can change rapidly and dramatically and these changes often require major changes in a company's strategic plan. There are several articles which provide examples of companies that came to grief because of adherence to a plan which changing circumstances had made obsolete."

The plans you will make for implementing DIGS in your company will in all likelihood provide very useful guides to the implementation. The insight you will gain into your business through the dissection and study of your marketing processes will prove invaluable.

In this chapter, we look at a spectrum of planning tools—Pro formas to predict financial results, contact plans to decide the nature and frequency of your communications, and BASIC, our acronym for crafting practical, effective offers to customers and prospects. We show how to employ all these tools of the DIGS to make sure your marketing efforts will generate appropriate sales and profits.

Developing Pro Formas

Pro formas are established tools in direct marketing. They have helped to guide the marketing efforts of catalog retailers, magazine publishers, record and book clubs, and many other direct marketers for decades. You can learn a valuable lesson adopting their discipline. Competition is tougher, your markets have expanded to include all regions of the world, and advances in technology are now providing opportunities in markets that you have never seen before.

Fifteen years ago, it wasn't cost-effective to air freight fresh flowers from South America to Europe or ship used tires from Seattle to Shanghai. Today, it's someone's thriving business. Companies are also better at innovating, more focused on gaining technological edges, and quicker to react to attack from other firms. Today, it's tougher to gain product-based superiority than in years past.

But product-based superiority isn't enough, anymore. What you really need to generate long-term sustained competitive strength is customer-based superiority. And that's also tougher than ever. New markets emerge continually in previously overlooked regions and markets. As a marketer, your margins are likely to come under severe pressure and your budgets are likely to be scrutinized even as you are expected to market to more prospects and customers than ever. There's a dichotomy there—the one this book is built around. Our goal is to teach you how to use technology and information and proven techniques to better integrate your sales and marketing efforts allowing you to build a sustainable customer-based advantage over your competitors.

One thing that hasn't changed is every marketer's need to ensure that his or her efforts achieve their desired results. Famed retailer John Wanamaker may have been able to get away with saying,

"I know I'm wasting half my advertising; I just don't know which half." That was a long time ago and you can't afford such luxuries any longer. Today, every dollar counts and every dollar must be accounted for.

Pro formas provide your best tools for accurately budgeting amounts adequate for attracting new prospects and upgrading existing customers by taking into account the eventual profits or lack of profits that may result from the expenditure of that budget.

Despite their power, pro formas aren't as widely utilized as you might think. We found this out one day when we were making a presentation to a division controller and his staff. We ran through our pro forma, outlining what our proposed marketing campaign was going to cost and the sales we projected it would generate. Nothing in this exercise was particularly unusual. But, to our surprise, the controller fell completely silent. It was the first time in the company's history, he told us, that someone had logically and coherently predicted sales before actually spending the money to execute a campaign. This executive was thrilled to have this financial tool in his hands and so will you.

The building blocks of a pro forma are assumptions based on past test results or on estimates (Figure 5.1). Here is a set of assumptions you might utilize to create a basic pro forma that documents your allowable budget, your projected units to be sold, and the allowable number of communications you can execute throughout the campaign.

- *Unit Revenue.* This figure represents the revenue you will collect for each unit sold. In Figure 5.1, the unit price is $15,000. Typically, a higher end item like this can justify a higher quantity of marketing money per unit.
- *Percent of Revenue Allowed.* An amount you have selected to represent the maximum amount of the revenue per unit that can be

Figure 5.1 Marketing Pro Forma

Allowable Budget	Assumptions
• Unit revenue	$ 15,000
• Percent of revenue allowed	5%
• Budget per unit	$ 750
Budget Allocation	
• Targets	250,000
• Response rates	3%
• Close rates	35%
• Units sold	2,625
• Promotion budget	$1,968,750
• Average times promoted	3
• Allowable promo/person	$ 2.63

devoted to marketing. This number is generated from your profit and loss statement based on your knowledge of your own costs in conjunction with your specific corporate objectives for sales growth and profit margins.

- *Budget per Unit.* This gives you the amount of money you can spend to market each unit. It's calculated by multiplying the Unit Revenue by the Percent of Revenue Allowed.

Budget per Unit = Unit Revenue × Percent of Revenue Allowed

- *Targets.* This is the number of customers and prospects you will attempt to reach with your offer. You will arrive at this number by selecting segments from your Value Segmentation Matrix—typically selecting your most strategic or valuable customers and prospects.
- *Response Rate.* The projected percent of people receiving your offer who will respond positively. The response may be to take advantage of a trial subscription, agree to receive a sales call, or other behavior. Response rates can vary widely—ranging from less than 1 percent to more than 40 percent, depending on many

factors. One of the most important variables is your audience. Are you marketing to existing customers or new prospects? Established clients typically yield higher response rates; new prospects generally produce lower results. What response rate should you use? It's hard to say. Too much depends on the offer to answer precisely. A 2 percent response rate would be very good for some offers to some segments, very poor for others. To come up with the answer you'll need, look at what happened with past promotions of similar offers to similar segments. Use in-house figures where possible, and buttress your assumptions with industry averages where you can.

- *Close Rate.* This is a projection of the percentage of responders who will eventually make a purchase resulting from this offer. As with response rate, Close Rate will vary widely. You will have to make your best guess as to what percentage of responders will become buyers. Again, if you look to past history, your best guess can be quite accurate.
- *Units Sold.* You arrive at this projection by multiplying the number of responders by the Close Rate. In Figure 5.1, 3 percent of 250,000 is 7,500 and 35 percent of 7,500 is 2,625 units sold.
- *Promotion Budget.* Generate this number by multiplying the number of Units Sold by the Allowable Budget per Unit. In Figure 5.1, it's 2,625 units sold times $750, yielding a $1,968,750 budget for promotion. Often you will work backward from this figure, using it to decide such things as how many people you will attempt to contact, how many units can be expected to be sold given your existing marketing budget, and whether the planned selling price is adequate to support your required marketing effort.
- *Average Number of Times Promoted.* It's likely that you'll have to expose your message to your prospects more than once before you generate your desired behavior. This number drives your contact plan and represents the total number of times you will send the offer to each potential purchaser. Promotions may

consist of direct mail letters, phone calls, sales calls, e-mails, and other contacts.

- *Allowable Promotion Dollars per Person.* This number is derived by dividing the number of targets (250,000) into the Promotion Budget ($1,968,750) and then again by the Average Number of Times promoted. This is a key number because it will guide how much you can spend on designing and printing materials for mailing, scripting and conducting telemarketing calls, and sending live salespeople on calls.

These are by no means all the components of a comprehensive pro forma. *Basic pro forma components should incorporate the drivers of your marketing and sales efforts, including all items that you want to measure.* Additional assumptions you may want to include are Units per Order and Total Number of Orders Needed. You may want to have Close Rates only for those contacted who are interested and motivated. You may have separate entries for different types of responses, such as expressed interest, requested sample, made purchase, and so on. You could separate customers from prospects and further divide customers into two categories—new customers or established buyers.

You are likely to use and account for more than one medium, including direct mail, telemarketing, e-mail, sales calls, and dimensional mail. In addition to multiple contacts, you may engage in multiple campaigns, preparing a pro forma to help manage each of them. Some pro formas include a percentage of the cost paid to an agency or in-house person to create the material. Other costs include printing, postage, order processing and other mail, production, and fulfillment costs.

A sophisticated pro forma may take into account return rates, gross margins, and operating expenses to arrive at a figure for net profits. It may include additional income from service revenues, name rental revenues, and referral revenues. In this way, the Direct Impact Growth System can become a primary tool for managing your business, not just your marketing.

The role of pro formas is vitally important for, among other things, the fact that they set the stage for sales' execution. A well-designed pro forma can show an individual sales agent that 33 percent of his territory's quota will come from current accounts. This means that more than two-thirds of his time and efforts must be focused on new prospects. Living off of your customer base won't provide you with a ticket to the annual 100 percent club. Pro formas can be tied to the company's overall financial forecast, yet easily articulated and understood at the sales territory level. Done properly, a pro forma can yield the target number of customers, prospects, and units each sales representative should be responsible for. The importance of this cannot be overstated. Nothing accelerates sales execution like clear, concise, and personal objectives.

Creating Contact Plans

Reach out and touch someone. It sounds pretty simple and, after all, it is the foundation of any successful sales and marketing effort. But executing this simple directive is not so simple. Take the case of one large business-to-business marketer we consulted with. Its marketing universe consisted of more than 60,000 customer and prospect sites—not itself an unmanageable number. But consider that there were an average of 10 people at each of those sites, from CEO to end user, that we had to communicate with, and it's easy to see that things quickly get more complicated. Furthermore, the company wanted to use mail, e-mail, telemarketing, and sales calls to get their message across. Also the company didn't want to treat all those customers and prospects the same—Value Segmentation is, after all, the basis of the Direct Impact Growth System strategy. Instead, it selected its audience from its Value Segmentation Matrix and devoted an appropriate amount of resources to each group, making sure to focus more resources on those targets that were expected to yield high returns to the company.

Place yourself in tomorrow's staff meeting. How would you handle the above campaign? What pieces are in place that would allow you to address the problem?

In the Direct Impact Growth System, how you contact your target segments, and what the expected results of those contacts will be, is contained in the Contact Plan you prepare for each marketing campaign. The Contact Plan (Figure 5.2) answers major questions such as: How am I going to contact these targets? What media will I use? How often should I contact them?

Contact plans guide you in selecting how and how often you plan to touch base with your selected customers and prospects.Contact plans help you allocate the dollars in your marketing budget to specific segments and promotion efforts.

Notice that the amounts from the pro forma—number of names promoted to, total marketing budget, units sold, and so forth— all match up with the numbers on this Contact Plan. You are marketing to three distinct segments, using a different number and mix of contacts for each segment. You are allocating a different amount of money to each person in each segment and each segment overall. The projected response rates are also different for each sector, vary-

Figure 5.2 Contact Plan (M = Mail, E = E-mail, C = Call, P = Presentation)

Segment	$$$	$$	$	Totals
Contacts	MMECP	MECP	MM	$ 3.18
Circulation	10,000	65,000	145,000	250,000
Budget/Name	$ 13.13	$ 10.50	$ 5.25	$ 2.63
Budget/Segment	$525,200	$682,500	$761,250	$1,968,950
Response/Segment	6.00%	2.50%	2.00%	2.77%
Close/Segment	35%	35%	35%	35%
Units	840	796	1,015	2,651

ing by a factor of three. Yet the number of contacts per person, while varying from two to five, when added together equals the total number of contacts bottom line that generate the number of units sold you need to sell. This is how you come up with a Contact Plan that is intended to meet your business goals.

Behind the seeming simplicity of a Contact Plan lies considerable complexity, ranging from the rationale you used to select the segments you attacked to assumptions you used for your response rates and close rates. Let's examine the elements of a Contact Plan more closely:

- *Select Segments.* The three segment labels—$$$, $$, $—are shorthand for the emphasis placed on the three value segments chosen by the marketers behind this Contact Plan. The $$$ segment is the group most likely to provide future growth. These targets may have large budgets but presently buy little or not at all from us. They are, essentially, the most promising prospects. They have the farthest to go to become loyal, high-volume customers, but they have a lot to offer once we bring them into the fold. Logically, they receive the most contacts and are allocated the largest per-person portion of the marketing budget. The $$ segment is also important. It is a significantly larger group that, with a considerably smaller contact budget per name and a response rate less than half the $$$ segment, will produce nearly as many sales. Significant attention will be paid to this group. The $ segment is by far the largest, both in terms of numbers and contribution to sales. Without a pro forma, a marketer may spend an amount equal to the value of a $$$ group, and then he is overspending. In Figure 5.2, the marketer knows he will spend less here than in any other value segment. The cost per sale in this group is much higher and that must be taken into account. Members of the $ segment, however, may not offer the promise of growth presented by the $$$ and $$ groups. The marketer knows this and takes this into consideration.

- *Contacts.* The MECP codes in the Contacts column, standing for mail, e-mail, call, and presentation, describe the manner in which you will contact your targets. Mail is the tried-and-true direct marketing standby. Multiple contacts are normally used in direct marketing involving mail simply because it is difficult to sell anything through a single contact. E-mail is an evolving alternative that is much less costly than regular mail. Call is short for a telemarketing contact, useful for qualifying leads and scheduling sales calls as well as closing some sales. Presentation refers to a full-blown sales call, the most costly form of contact and reserved for the best-qualified, most-interested prospects. The five-contact MMECP scheme for the $$$ segment stands for two mailings followed by an e-mail, a phone call, and, finally, a live sales presentation. In keeping with the $$$ theme, this illustrates a steady ramping up of intensity on increasingly better-selected prospects. It's important to share this Contact Plan with your salesforce, so that they will know how and when to engage. Nor should you limit yourself to the MECP contacts described in this sample plan. For instance, you may employ fax messages, executive briefings, Web page launches, or other contacts. Mass advertising can also play a role if you are sure of the reach. We'll cover sales preparation and execution in Step 8.
- *Circulation.* This number describes the targeted quantity of names in each value segment. It is significant because, given the 250,000 universe limitation, each value segment can only carve out for its own a limited portion of that total. Further, given the considerable variation in cost per person of contacts for members of each value segment, your budget is highly sensitive to the Circulation of each segment.
- *Budget per Name.* This entry is dependent on the number and type of contacts specified in the Contacts box. More Contacts obviously cost more, and sales presentations obviously cost a lot more than all the other types of Contacts. Budget per Name is,

therefore, determined by the number and types of Contacts. Note that the $2.63 overall budget for Contacts per Name remains intact and is the same figure as that cited in the pro forma.

- *Budget per Segment.* This is simply Circulation times the Budget per Name. Notice that the numbers for Budget per Segment add up to the same figure as was presented for the total marketing budget in the pro forma.
- *Response per Segment.* This is a number of critical importance that, unfortunately, cannot be precisely determined in advance. It's going to vary widely depending on the accuracy and freshness of the data in your database, the power and appeal of your offer, and many other factors.
- *Close per Segment.* Like Response per Segment, this number can only be determined by looking at what has happened in the past and extrapolating forward. Basically, you examine the results of past campaigns and assume that the results from this one will be similar. Be sure to adjust for any important differences in the campaigns, such as offer price or market environment. Bear in mind, since conditions never exactly replicate themselves, you will never be perfectly precise on this number.
- *Units.* The number of units you expect to sell is calculated by multiplying Circulation times Response per Segment times Close per Segment. For the $$$ segment, for instance, the figure of 840 is 35 percent of 6 percent of 40,000, or 40,000 times 0.06 times 0.35. Note that the total units sold, 2,651, is the same as the number from the pro forma.

All the elements of a Contact Plan interlink to form a coherent whole. You can't change any part of the Contact Plan without changing another, or you will have an effect on the Plan's bottom line, as well as the pro forma. Given that the sales figure is the end result you are focusing on, the Contact Plan can be described as a holistic approach in which the various elements depend on and reinforce each other in pursuit of a common goal. The individual elements of the Contact Plan are neither casual nor haphazard. Rather, they are carefully calculated components of an elaborate system, each part of which has to be properly tuned for the system to do its job. They are the drivers of your business, or at least your marketing efforts.

Creating BASIC Impact Offers

Everybody is awash in "special," "limited-time only," and "preferred customer" offers—to name just a few catchphrases The generic "everybody" we speak of here unfortunately includes your customers as well. Given the overcrowded, confusing world of marketing messages, what can you do to make sure the offers you extend are as outstanding and effective as possible? We have developed an approach to crafting high-impact offers we call BASIC (Figure 5.3).

BASIC stands for Believable, Achievable, Sustainable, Interesting, and Compelling, which represent the elements of the most effective offers at generating the all-important customer or prospect response.

Just For Feet, a warehouse-style athletic shoe retailer in the southern half of the United States, makes an unusual offer to all its customers and prospects. If you purchase a dozen pairs of shoes, you get the 13th pair free. It's an eye-catching offer at first glance—who doesn't like the idea of something for free? But, when the rubber meets the road, it turns out to be something less than a real toe-tapper of an offer to the broad market they target. The problem is that it's not Believable. Think about it—when was the last time you bought a dozen pairs of athletic shoes? If you're like most people, a dozen pairs represents years' worth of shoe purchases for you. So, although Just For Feet, undoubtedly gets a few prospects to check it out on the basis of this free-pair offer, only exceptionally high-mileage joggers and heads of unusually large families are likely

Figure 5.3 BASIC™ Impact

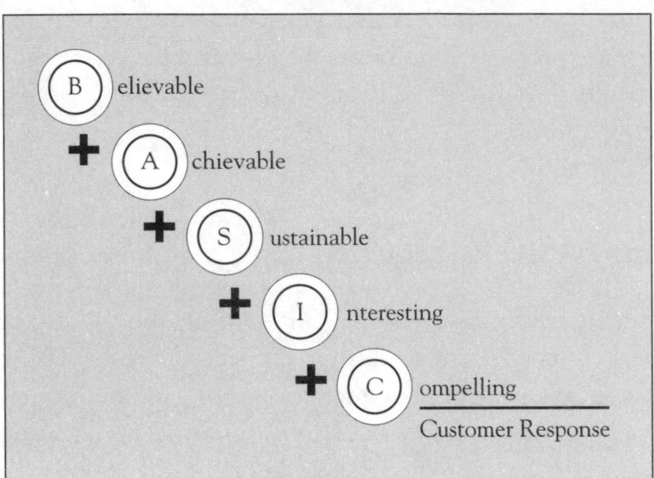

to ever be able to take advantage of this offer. This offer fails on the second criterion of the BASIC template: Achievability. Here is how the elements of the BASIC offer stack up:

- *Believable.* The most elemental appeal of an offer is that it be credible. The prospect has to be willing to accept that the offer is for real and will be fulfilled. Rather than cooking up a superficially interesting but ultimately unbelievable offer, make sure your offer is more like the one from *Natural History* magazine. If you subscribe to *Natural History* for $22, it comes with a free pass to visit the New York City museum, a discount on tickets to an IMAX movie, and discounts on purchases from the museum's gift shop. This is a believable offer.
- *Achievable.* Many vendors offer to enter customers and prospects in sweepstakes to win cash prizes, new cars, and so on. However, people who are not inclined to buy something anyway may not flock to make a purchase in order to enter a sweepstakes where the stated odds of winning are probably in excess of a million-to-one. This offer fails because, in the mind of the customer, it's not

an achievable offer. Much better was the one we recently received from a local Honda dealer. The dimensional mailer contained a key. If it opened the locked door of a brand-new Accord sitting on the dealer's lot, you were entitled to drive away in that same car. The stated odds on the flyer accompanying the key were 1 in 3,000—not enough to make a special trip perhaps, but worth sauntering over and trying your key if you happened to be in that part of town.

- *Sustainable.* Now let's look at the offer from your perspective. Obviously, you have to be able to make good on an offer for your projected number of respondents or it's not a good one. The computer manufacturer who offered customers a free server for every two desktop PCs ordered was not making a sustainable offer. The motivation for the offer was clear enough: The manufacturer found itself overstocked with servers and figured it could clear the warehouse by giving some away to desktop buyers. This could have been a solid offer if the company was prepared to continue giving away servers or if it time stamped the offer by making it available for a limited time only or by limiting the number of free servers each customer could receive. But in this case, there was a seriously constrained supply of these servers and, in the absence of controls or compensating requirements, giving away a high-margin server to the buyer of two low-margin PCs was not a sustainable business practice. Because it was not sustainable, this offer gets a bad BASIC grade. Other factors may figure into sustainability. For instance, you want to be able to test and learn from any offer. An offer that doesn't provide you with this capability may not meet your long-term goals and, ultimately, prove unsustainable.

  A better offer was available from a handheld computer maker. Anybody who purchased a particular Palm handheld computer and subscribed to Palm's wireless Internet for a year got $100 back. This was clearly a sustainable offer, since Palm was getting a significant commitment from the user. The minimum fee to sign up for a year's service was $120, slightly more than the rebate but not so much that the user would feel the offer was not worth taking advantage of. It should be pointed out that this offer probably makes sense from Palm's perspective only if the company can comfortably predict renewal rates of its wireless service. As an introductory offer, this might be too risky to sustain. But, if the company knows the renewal rates are high, this might be a great offer that attracts a bevy of new customers.

- *Interesting.* This one is a little slippery because what one person finds interesting bores another. But a good example of an often-interesting proposition is to send out a postcard inviting a customer or prospect to shop a private sale a day before the public is invited to partake in it. The idea that you might get a shot at a sale item before anybody else even knows about it is usually interesting to many people.
- *Compelling.* Book clubs have refined the compelling offer to a high level. Who hasn't done a double-take on seeing the envelope of a direct-mail letter from a book club offering four books for $1 or 12 free books just for joining the club? These offers, if not irresistible, are at least compelling to prompt a closer look from many in their target segments.

The BASIC impact framework can be used to craft offers in many sorts of media, including e-mail, bulk direct mail, high-end direct mail, telemarketing, Web activities, and mass advertising. Planning an effective BASIC offer requires knowing what matters to the segment you are contacting, plus knowing your own capabilities as a business.

Facts to Remember

- ❀ Pro formas provide you with a tool to accurately estimate your marketing campaign's budget, performance, and results.
- ❀ Basic Pro forma components should incorporate the drivers of your marketing and sales efforts, including all items that you want to measure.
- ❀ Contact Plans guide you in selecting how and how often you plan to touch base with selected segments of your customers and prospects. Contact Plans help you allocate the dollars in your marketing budget to specific segments and promotion efforts.
- ❀ BASIC stands for Believable, Achievable, Sustainable, Interesting, and Compelling—the elements of the most effective offers at generating the all-important customer or prospect response.

STEP

6

Organizational Magnification

When Janet started working on Mercedes-Benz it was clear that the main players—corporate headquarters in Germany, the U.S. headquarters, and the North American dealer network—were not on the same page regarding customer handling and product messaging.

Germany remained steadfast in its old-line messaging of safety and engineering. The U.S. corporate headquarters knew that the marque needed some new energy and was turning out television commercials featuring Janis Joplin singing, "Oh Lord, won't you buy me a Mercedes-Benz." The dealer network would say whatever seemed appropriate to get a sale.

The poor customer was trying to figure out who the company was and what they should expect from the "Mercedes-Benz experience," as it was called.

For the first time in its history, Mercedes-Benz was losing customer loyalty. This, in large measure, was due to a lack of understanding of a concept we call *Organizational Magnification*.

Organizational Magnification refers to the process that results in getting everyone working together on the same Direct Impact Growth System plan. The idea is to integrate the company around a Market Management System by prepping salespeople and others on the goals, strategy, and methods that are part of the program, explaining their roles in the effort and convincing them to participate fully. Organizational Magnification means getting the whole company to understand, focus, and execute against a clear set of corporate objectives, saying the same thing and behaving the same way.

Organization Magnification derives its power from a couple of sources. The first is the simple leveraging effect of teamwork. If your people are working together on the same plan in pursuit of the same objectives, the whole adds up to more than the parts. If they aren't, you might as well not have a plan. Your efforts will be far less effective unless you can get everyone working together.

Clear, concise communication is the grease that lubricates your marketing engine. Throughout this step, we'll talk to you about how to present your campaign strategy and how to explain the individual components of your marketing program. We'll discuss how to organize a crisp executive summary that accurately describes your program's activities and objectives. We help you articulate your strategy, reinforce your message, and select your targets. We'll show you a blueprint you can follow to successfully prepare and motivate your sales team to execute against your objectives.

An important component of Organizational Magnification is that everyone in the company begins to understand and implement the power of uniformity; talking and behaving the same way to customers and prospects. This creates an exceptionally powerful multiplying effect when it comes to marketing. It's well known that multiple exposures to a marketing message increase its effectiveness.

When any customer or prospect gets the same consistent message each time he or she comes in contact with anyone at your company, it's the same as if you sent him or her multiple marketing messages. The consistency made possible by Organizational Magnification lets a company enjoy a compounding effect on marketing.

Customer Attack Plan

Once your market's Value Segmentation Matrix is complete, decisions must be made about the best way for your organization to approach each one of your customers and prospects. These are difficult decisions and, depending on the specific situation that your company is facing, you may develop or change your approach to maximize short-term revenue or pursue a path that minimizes competitive threats within your strategic accounts. The direction you take must be clearly communicated so that everyone has a clear understanding of the company's mission and purpose. The central document that outlines your overall strategy, objectives, and tactical plans is what we call a Customer Attack Plan or CAP.

The Customer Attack Plan seeks to answer and explain how you will deploy your marketing and sales resources to optimize results while minimizing costs. As with all elements of a Direct Impact Growth System, a CAP focuses on specific goals, strategies, and resources to come up with an actionable, understandable plan tailored to help you achieve your corporate objectives.

You will work with the Value Segmentation Matrix to help you decide how to draw up your customer CAP. For instance, your CAP may call for you first to work on customers ranked on the order of their estimated IT budget, high-budget customers first, low-budget customers next. In a typical Value Segmentation Matrix, high-budget customers would be found in the top row of boxes, with low-budget customers occupying the bottom row. Next, you may decide to rank them on the share of wallet you own in each customer, dealing with high-share customers first and saving low-share customers for later on. In a Value Segmentation Matrix, high-share and high-budget customers would be found in the topmost square in the righthand column. A CAP is just as flexible as the Value Segmentation Matrix. For example, you may further allocate your resources based on how your salesforce is distributed. Do you have salespeople in place to conveniently service some customers and prospects but not others? Does a certain account have marquee value that could influence others to buy your product if you can get them on board?

Your CAP may recognize any number of criteria. For example, while Patrick was in sales at IBM, one of the IBM salespeople developed a very good approach for selling against one of our competitors. This approach was a simple but highly structured step-by-step process for identifying and exploiting specific weaknesses in the competitor's products and services. When Patrick applied the recommended approach on three of his competitor's accounts in his territory, he converted two of them. Competitive opportunities may be factors to consider when mapping out your attack strategies.

Given that one of the main uses of your plan is as a communications tool, a good executive summary is an important part of any CAP. The plan's Executive Summary should take up no more than a few pages of paper or slides in a show and should include the following elements:

- Synopsis of your overall strategy.
- Overview of your marketing budget.
- Description of how you are going to integrate roles and responsibilities.
- Summary discussion of the information you selected from your Market Development System database.
- Discussion of your campaign strategy.
- Description and examples of your marketing message.

- Defined listing of accounts that you are targeting.
- Overview of the different marketing vehicles you are going to use in your campaign.
- A diagram outlining how and when the different components of your campaign will be executed.

Let's begin our discuss with a synopsis of your overall strategy.

Strategy Synopsis. Describe the basic strategy you are following in your marketing plan. Try to be as specific as possible without getting bogged down in details. Since this summary is for executives, center your discussion on the things they will be interested in—strategy, resources, costs, and expected revenues. Avoid overgeneralizations.

Here's an example of an overly general strategy synopsis:

> Core Concepts Inc. intends to be the No. 1 provider of marketing solutions to the Fortune 500.

This is a grandiose objective that any marketer would be hard-pressed to implement. Your strategy synopsis is not meant to be a restatement of your company's mission statement but your strategy should support your company's overall vision and purpose. Leave out the hype. Speak plainly about limitations and how you plan to overcome them. Here's a better example:

> Core Concepts sees the Fortune 500 as the most likely purchasers of our solutions. However, we lack the broad industry experience to market effectively to all large corporations. Therefore, we are concentrating our efforts on consumer product companies in the personal care sector. A concentrated direct mail campaign to decision makers at these companies, followed by telemarketing and sales presentations, will allow us to have a bigger impact in these more focused markets.

Budget. The first thing any internal person is going to wonder about your marketing plan is: How much is this going to cost? Some companies tend to be secretive about marketing budgets, restricting information about them to those who "need to know." However, the principle of Organizational Magnification is that everybody needs to know. So answer this inevitable question by stating plainly what you plan to spend and how you plan to spend it. Offer dollar amounts, timing, and geographic and media details as well.

Here's an example of a good budget section in an executive strategy summary:

> We will be investing approximately $150,000 in the personal care sector. All of these marketing dollars will be expended in the third quarter. The budget will cover direct mail, telemarketing, and sales presentations made to target companies as follows:
>
> - $40,000 will be spent on direct mail to all target companies.
> - $60,000 will be spent on telemarketing to mail respondents and key accounts.
> - $50,000 will be spent on sales calls to qualified and key accounts.

Your budget review can play a valuable role in winning over reluctant salespeople. Point out to any salespeople who seem slow to get with the program: "I'm investing marketing dollars in your territory and in you. I'm spending money and working to make you more successful." By positioning yourself as an ally to sales, you are also setting the stage for accountability. If you have made a significant investment in their success, you are entitled to make the same request of them.

Integration. Now is the time to point out that other functions—specifically, sales—will have key roles to play in making this marketing effort successful. Don't just declare that sales' participation will be important. Offer concise descriptions of how sales and marketing will work together.

Here is an example of integration:

Direct mail and telemarketing and a limited amount of mass advertising will be used to raise awareness in the target market as well as obtain and qualify leads for salespeople to follow up on. Integration will occur in the following fashion:

- Direct mail will be used to raise awareness and generate buyer responses.
- Telemarketing calls will be made to accounts responding to direct mail.
- Sales calls will be made to accounts qualified by telemarketing.

One-way sharing of information may not always be enough to generate support among salespeople. So make it a two-way flow. Ask, encourage, and require salespeople to join the process and provide their own input. For example, provide them with sample telemarketing scripts and ask them if they have ideas for improving the scripts. Point out that they are the closest to the customers, and know best how to approach them. Once you include input from your sales team in the marketing materials, you will find it much easier to get them to buy into the campaign.

Describe Your Market Development System Database. The database of information you are building will play a vital part in your marketing campaigns, present and future. Describe, briefly, this database's purpose, contents, and uses. For instance, a DIGS database might be described as intended to provide accurate and detailed information about our customers, prospects, and suspects to enable our sales teams to identify and create new business opportunities, enhance relationships with current accounts, increase site and product penetration with targeted accounts, and drive revenue, units, and margin.

You can best describe the database components and contents by naming logical items that your audience can understand. Don't be too skimpy here, however. What you are doing is laying out the tools of sales success. You are illustrating tangible investments and tools to help the sales process. The more your sales team understands and appreciates this database, the more use they will be able to make of it.

After the Executive Summary, a Customer Attack Plan (CAP) can and should go into greater detail. You will have separate sections providing more information on:

- Campaign strategy,
- Your message and the logic and associate proof points behind it,
- Target markets,
- Marketing media (direct mail, advertising, telemarketing, etc.) you will be using in the campaign, and
- How the program will flow, or how the marketing and sales efforts will fit together.

Exactly how far you will go with detailing a particular edition of the plan depends on what you want to use it for. In its barest form, a CAP may be suitable for a quick presentation at a company meeting to give your employees an understanding of the activities that are going to occur over the life of the campaign. At the other end, when it comes to communicating the duties of sales and marketing personnel, your CAP will be far more extensive and detailed, down to describing planned air times for specific radio ads and individual salespeople's responsibility for following up on contacts at target customers.

Campaign Plan

The details of your Campaign Plan should include your overall goal, the role of the critical database of information in your plan, rudiments of how sales and marketing will be integrated, and any special features of the plan. To introduce some of the ideas behind developing a plan, however, Figure 6.1 is a sample plan derived from

Figure 6.1 Example of a Campaign Plan

Campaign Plan

1. Dominate Target Market Media for Four-Week Period
   - Deliver compelling messages via multiple media.
   - Mix targeted sales efforts with mass efforts to insure frequency.
2. Use Market Management System to Arm Salesforce with Detailed Account Information
   - Provide territory and contact management reports.
   - Generate summarized account profile information on selected accounts.
3. Integrate Sales and Marketing to Insure Proper Development and Execution
   - Distribute prerelease copies of advertisements, radio scripts, and direct mail.
   - Follow-up with written and e-mail correspondence.
   - Create sales scripts for telephone follow-up.
4. Develop Special Messages for Each Local Market
   - Custom advertisements and telephone scripts by geography.
   - Unique URL addresses for each city.

an actual CAP that includes four areas of emphasis and major elements of each.

Figure 6.1 is a special case, representing a company that was the third-largest player in its market and had previously spent heavily on advertising with poor results. The details of a Campaign Plan will vary considerably from company to company.

For purposes of Organizational Magnification, the important thing about presenting your Campaign Plan is to impart to your employees the vision of a well thought-out, carefully choreographed marketing and sales effort. Individual salespeople, marketers, customer service reps, and others should be armed with a consistent message they can present to customers and prospects.

Everyone should feel confident performing their roles in executing this plan, knowing what the end result is to be and how they can affect it. The next sections will further that understanding of personal contributions to overall corporate success in the context of the Direct Impact Growth System.

Message

When Organizational Magnification is working well, everyone in the whole company is expressing the same message to every customer and prospect. How can this come about? After all, a marketing message is more than a slogan. If Organizational Magnification is to work as well as it can, everyone has to understand the message in detail, and be ready to respond to questions and even objections, rather than just spouting a marketing motto. Making sure everyone understands the message that is to be presented to customers and prospects will help ensure that no one acts or speaks out of harmony with that message, and will encourage them to find ways to elaborate and amplify it in their dealing in the marketplace. In the message portion of your Customer Attack Plan, summarize the message's main point in a headline-style statement. Follow up with the thinking behind the message—the implications of your message and

Figure 6.2 Customer Attack Plan Message Template

Message	
Implications	
Proof Points	

Figure 6.3 Customer Attack Plan Message

Message	• Saving $100 a month on a $39.95 high-speed Internet service—hype or hope?
Implications	• The message is intended to provide a reaction: • Recipients will identify with both answers, while hoping it's not hype. • The rest of the message will prove it's not hype, we can deliver.
Proof Points	• The ISPs award-winning customer service reduces operating costs. • Industry-standard uptime record slashes downtime, increases productivity. • Preconfigured service defaults expediate installation.

why you selected it. Finish with the proof that backs up your claim. Figure 6.2 is a template for a CAP message. Figure 6.3 is a message template for an Internet service provider with all blanks filled in. This message explanation tells people in your organization what the message is, what targets' reactions to it are likely to be, and how the campaign will substantiate the claims it sets up. For salespeople and telemarketers, detailed scripts would be written to explain and articulate these core proof points in pursuit of actual sales. For others in the organization, closing a sale isn't the objective. Don't forget to provide your receptionists and delivery people with messages. Change your on-hold music or building entry signs if appropriate as well. The end result is a satisfying setup and close that engenders understanding, confidence, and the ability to present a cohesive message and followthrough to customers and prospects by everybody in the organization. That is the essence of Organizational Magnification.

Targets

In addition to covering the message you're getting out, your Customer Attack Plan should include a profile of your target audience.

The profiles targeted in your Customer Attack Plan will be selected using the Value Segmentation Matrix. Now take some of the details describing those value segments and make the people in your company aware of the characteristics of your target groups. For instance, if you are marketing family medical insurance plans, your targets might be middle- and upper-income households in which the primary wage earner is self-employed and there are minor children at home. Explain also how these targets were selected—self-employed people aren't as likely to be covered by other medical insurance as corporate employees, childless households aren't as concerned about health care costs and the income levels are chosen to make sure the targets can afford the premiums. You don't have to get extremely detailed here, however. Just let the people in your company know who will be on the receiving end of your marketing campaign and why.

Also include information about geographical targets. If you're segmenting your campaign by metropolitan areas, for instance, let people in your company know in which ZIP codes direct mail pieces, radio ads, or other media are going to hit. This will necessarily have to be pretty detailed with regard to integrating telemarketing and sales calls as follow-ups to other marketing deliveries. The rest of the organization can be presented with the broad outline of the territories you're going to attack. Once again, however, explain the rationale behind the target geography. If you are marketing to a limited region, point out that this lets you concentrate your resources. If you selected specific metropolitan areas because of the relative absence of effective competitors there, say so. Providing reasons for doing what you do will enrich and deepen the understanding of the marketing campaign and lead to a higher degree of Organizational Magnification.

Media Plan

You should communicate your media plan in terms both marketing and nonmarketing personnel can relate to. For example, one plan might be expressed as follows:

Media Plan

- Employ stair-step exposure.
- Generate quick burst of awareness via use of multiple media.
- Reduce media presence after first week.
- Use relationship-building tools on key accounts.
- Free tickets to theater and sporting events.
- All-expenses paid invitation to key customer seminar at resort location.

Knowing your plan for the marketing campaign helps everybody know what their job is in executing it. Equally important, it gives them guidelines about what *not* to do. For example, if they understand that relationship-building giveaways are restricted to key accounts, they won't talk up the offers to the smaller customers and prospects for which the offers are not intended. Specifics eliminate confusion, so be as specific as possible when outlining your media and promotional strategies.

Vehicles

One of the best ways to give your sales and marketing people an understanding of how you will pursue a given campaign is by telling them about the vehicles you will use. Explain all of the vehicles you are going to be using in your campaign. In our example, our marketer was going to be using radio and print advertisements backed by direct mail and a Web presence. This tells your employees where they can look for advertisements in the mass media, as well as where your customers and prospects are likely to see your message.

Recognize the morale-building effect on employees of seeing your marketing message. Once they begin to notice signs of your marketing, they'll think, "Hey! We're really doing something exciting in the marketplace." This generates a bandwagon effect that leverages Organizational Magnification.

You can get quite detailed in your information about vehicles. For instance, why not let everyone know when and on what stations your upcoming radio spots will run? If commuting employees can tune in to a company ad on a local radio station, or know where to look for an ad in their local newspaper, they will have participatory involvement in the campaign. Use direct mail to involve employees as well. *Seeding* is the practice of including in the mailing list some specific names and addresses of employees or other people with whom you can check to ascertain whether and when mailings were actually delivered. It can also provide feedback on how the packages appear mixed in with the rest of the mail in the real world.

Encourage employees to check out the campaign's Web promotion aspects. Ask them to critique your message and provide positive feedback on how quickly the pages loaded and what reactions the images you used evoked when they looked at them. You can get useful information about how easy your marketing materials are to find and how quickly pages load when viewed by a variety of users employing different types of modems and computers.

Program Flow

If you've ever seen a Rubik's Cube just out of the box or after someone has successfully arranged it so that each of the six sides shows just one color, it seems a simple thing. But just give it a few twists to mix up the colors, and try to put it back the way it was. You'll soon understand why more than 60 books have been written describing techniques for solving this devilishly intriguing and difficult puzzle. In the same way as Erno Rubik's inventive toy looks simple until you try to work it, it's one thing to be presented with all the details of a marketing campaign, and another to grasp how everything will fit together and the timing will work. In the Direct Impact Growth System, a Program Flow Chart provides crucial information about how the system works. Figure 6.4 is an example of a Program Flow Chart explaining the dates certain activities and media efforts will begin and showing how the following events play together.

Figure 6.4 Program Flow Chart

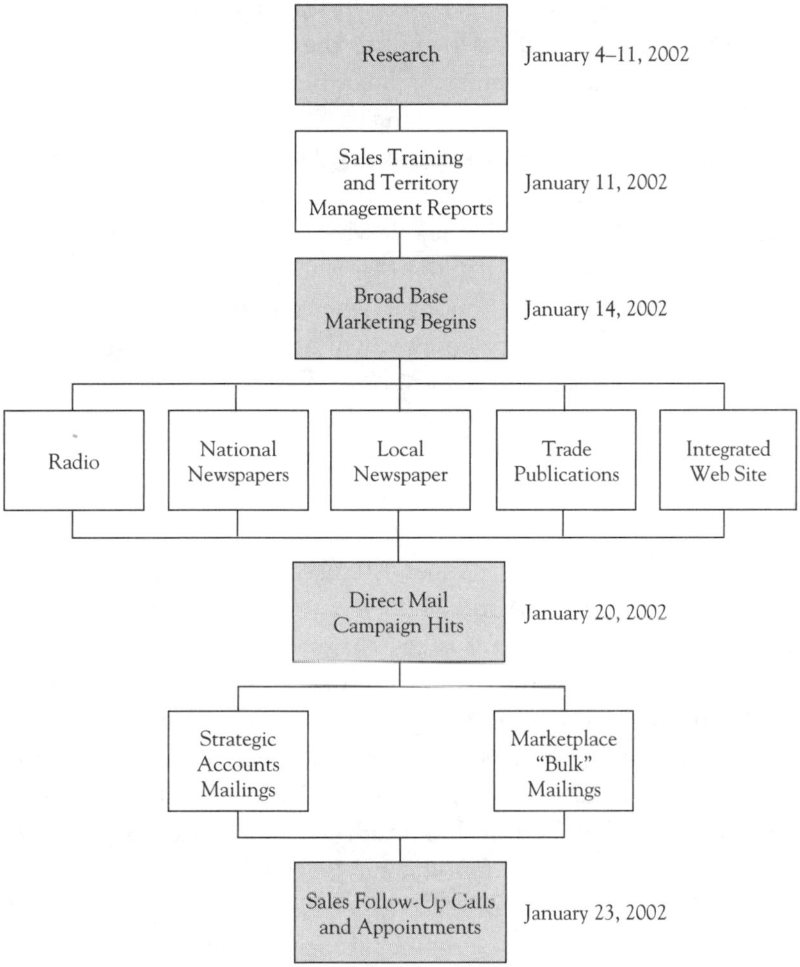

Research	January 4–11, 2002
Sales Training and Territory Management Reports	January 11, 2002
Broad Base Marketing Begins	January 14, 2002
Radio / National Newspapers / Local Newspaper / Trade Publications / Integrated Web Site	
Direct Mail Campaign Hits	January 20, 2002
Strategic Accounts Mailings / Marketplace "Bulk" Mailings	
Sales Follow-Up Calls and Appointments	January 23, 2002

Notice that the dates for the kickoffs of major program elements are included. Among other things, this explains why, for instance, salespeople shouldn't begin to make appointments until after mailings have occurred. It sets the stage for sales to clear their calendars of other, lower priority activities. If you don't provide this calendar information, you may well find yourself, as Patrick did, dealing with a district sales manager who had scheduled training for his team during the period just after a mailing when timing was optimum for making customer contacts. In this case, the sales manager had been prepped and rescheduling the training cleared up the matter. But you can minimize such conflicts by making sure everyone knows in advance what is going to happen and when. The Program Flow Chart also gives suggested dates for follow-up calls to begin happening and coordinates all activities in a sequential pattern so there is no confusion about what activities occur when and which activities your team should be working on now. It can help you plan ahead by letting you know when to expect Web hits or increased floor traffic. Program Flow will be looked at in greater detail in Step 7, Marketing Execution.

Customer Attack Plan

The ultimate idea of a Customer Attack Plan is to make sure that everyone involved knows how his or her efforts will contribute to the desired goal. When this is accomplished, Organizational Magnification will come into effect as every person in the company guides his or her work and customer interactions toward achieving the common objective. The customers will be attached not by individual salespeople, but by the combined potency of everyone in your company. The bottom-line results of even moderately successful Organizational Magnification can be startling.

Adaptec, the SCSI controller device company, found itself with stalled sales when Apple Computer stopped including hardware to support SCSI on the motherboards of Apple products. Adaptec needed a strong market campaign, but company executives didn't have a budget planned to cover it. They asked us to help them devise a plan that, for less than $100,000, could generate sales and move inventory.

We developed a channel attack plan that hit two titles in our target companies. We used direct mail, e-mail, white papers, a contest, t-shirts, sales materials, and scripts. We developed special Web pages for the Web site that reinforced the campaign. We trained all the sales representatives.

While we had a relatively small budget, we focused it and magnified it to the right set of customers. We ended up with a greater than 50 percent response. That's the power of Organizational Magnification. Visualize synchronized swimming and you've got it.

Facts to Remember

- Organizational Magnification refers to the process and the result of getting everyone working together on the same Direct Impact Growth System plan. The idea is to integrate the company around a Market Management System by prepping salespeople and others on the goals, strategy, and methods that are part of the program, explaining to them their roles in the effort and convincing them to participate fully. Organizational Magnification means getting the whole company to understand, focus, and execute against a clear set of corporate objectives, saying the same thing and behaving the same way.
- The Customer Attack Plan answers and explains how you will deploy your marketing and sales resources to optimize results while minimizing costs. As with all elements of a Direct Impact Growth System, a CAP focuses on specific goals, strategies, and resources to come up with an actionable, understandable plan tailored to help you achieve your corporate objectives.
- For purposes of Organizational Magnification, the important thing about presenting your Campaign Plan is to impart to your people the vision of a well thought-out, carefully choreographed marketing and sales effort. Individual salespeople, marketers, customer service reps, and

(Continued)

others should be armed with a consistent message they can present to customers and prospects.

- If Organizational Magnification is to work as well as it can, everyone has to understand the message in detail and be ready to respond to questions and even objections, rather than just spouting a marketing motto. Making sure everyone understands the message that is to be presented to customers and prospects will help ensure that no one acts or speaks out of harmony with that message, and will encourage them to find ways to elaborate and amplify it in their dealing in the marketplace.
- Knowing your plan for the marketing campaign helps everyone know what their job is in executing it. Equally important, it gives them guidelines about what not to do.
- Recognize the morale-building effect on employees of seeing your marketing message. Once they begin to notice signs of your marketing around them, they'll think, "Hey! We're really doing something exciting in the marketplace." This generates a bandwagon effect that leverages Organizational Magnification.

STEP

7

Marketing Execution

Any successful college student will tell you that to write a good term paper, you must first write an outline of what you want the paper to say. You draft how the paper will flow, the major points you want to make in the paper, and the supporting facts that substantiate the facts that you are communicating. In effect, your outline becomes the blueprint for your paper. By collecting and organizing your thoughts, the outline accelerates and consolidates your work, keeps you and your deadlines in balance, ultimately resulting in solid execution.

Marketing execution is no different. Crisp, competent completion of marketing's assignments is vital for a successful Direct Impact Growth System (DIGS) application. Marketing execution is the glue that holds it all together.

Before getting further into marketing execution, we want to make a couple of disclaimers. First, the responsibilities of the marketing department vary from company to company. Second, we are not trying to tell you how to manage your marketing department. These are the techniques that worked for us. They may work for you, *if* they fit your culture and organization.

We use the term *marketing play* to summarize the process of:

- Selecting segments most likely to contribute to specific corporate objectives,
- Building interest in those segments with direct mail and other communications,
- Equipping salespeople with information and tools to help reach those targets, and
- Integrating marketing activities with those of sales in a well-thought-out process moving from initial awareness through after-sale support.

Marketing plays are vital components of DIGS. Marketing Plays are highly goal-oriented, focused, well-organized, and coordinated efforts between sales and marketing. Before we get into the details of creating and executing your own marketing plays, Figure 7.1 is an example of a marketing play outline for a business-to-business information technology marketer making an offer for targets to evaluate a new product.

You don't have to be a team sports fan to appreciate the beauty of a well-executed play. When a hockey power play ties up all defenders leaving one scorer open for the winning goal, when a football team's pulling guard neatly clears out a cornerback so his halfback trots untouched into the end zone, or when a basketball fast break results in an uncontested lay up, spectators get a sense of satisfaction at watching a finely tuned group of people operating as a unit. Even fans of the opposing team have been known to give a standing ovation to an especially well orchestrated play. The same thing is true in activities as diverse as volleyball or bicycle racing—focusing a group's efforts on a predetermined goal can produce results so rapidly and smoothly that it appears effortless. Spectacular results don't usually occur, however, without the benefit of a well-thought-out plan and repetitive practice.

The Direct Impact Growth System can lead to similarly impressive results employing specific marketing plays. To continue the sports metaphor, marketing plays usually roll up into an overall

Figure 7.1 Marketing Play Outline

Buying Stages	Marketing Activities
Awareness	Direct mail to preselected value segments. Creation of dedicated pages. Telemarketing follow-ups to direct mail recipients.
Interest	Create introduction presentation kit and scripts for sales including: • Company overview • Products and services • Competitive advantages Prepare follow-up correspondence templates for: • Thank-you letters and e-mails • Confirmations • Scheduling presentations
Respond	Use sales tools: • Direct mail campaigns • Collateral materials • Customer presentation kits and scripts Use follow-up correspondence: • Reconfirming appointments e-mails • Telemarketing follow-up script • Product and services "benefits" letter • Thank-you letters and e-mails
Evaluate	Offer accepted option—if evaluation offer is accepted, engage in offer program, and follow up with sales and service activities. Offer declined without interest option—if evaluation offer is declined without interest, wait until the target expresses interest before recontacting. Offer declined with interest option—if evaluation offer is declined with interest, propose second conversation about other issues.
Buy	Follow up with those interested: • Direct mail • Event marketing • Web site access • Proactive sales presentation • Close Reengage decliners: • Direct mail • Event marketing • Web site access
Engage	Deepen customer engagements: • Specialized web site access • VIP conference • Product briefings

marketing game plan that maps out a variety of different activities to be executed by your team. Your goal as a professional marketer is to create a series of plays, within the context of your game plan, that emphasize your company's strengths while exploiting your competitors' weaknesses.

Marketing Plays

The idea behind a marketing play is to use the framework you have created to develop ongoing programs that are unique in the marketplace and that appeal to the audience. Marketing plays get their power from combining sales and marketing efforts to present cohesive messages at the right time to the right customer to illicit the desired behavior you are looking for. When designed and executed correctly, marketing plays are a key component of your Organization Magnification initiatives and serve to motivate your employees to a synchronized result.

Marketing plays come in several varieties. Each of these varieties is driven by business objectives, but each uses different methods to arrive at solutions. The main ones are:

- *Customer-Focused Marketing Plays* (CFMP) emphasize your relationship with the customer and targets using the Customer Relationship Continuum as $, $$, $$$, or some other series of titles—Conquest, Grow, and Own is one corresponding set that we have used. Different marketing plays would be developed and executed to address each group.
- *Product-Focused Marketing Plays* (PFMP) emphasize a specific product. Product-Focused Marketing Plays would be separated by product, such as desktop computers, notebooks, and servers or minivans, SUVs, and sedans. They are typically employed:
  —When a new product launches,
  —When a product is reaching the end of its market life,
  —For a seasonal effect such as the back-to-school clothes-buying season is about to become active, or

—At the end of a quarter or other sales period when corporate objectives or other measurements are tied to specific product sales.

You may also have marketing plays associated with specific channels. Additional marketing plays may be tied to events including:

- Trade shows,
- Web marketing efforts, and
- Collateral marketing plays.

A series of plays is gathered into a marketing play book that can be used to direct an entire campaign. Typically a play book incorporates the following information:

Section One: Business and Segment Management

A. Setting Quarterly Business Objectives
   a. Description
   b. Examples
      i. Revenue
      ii. Units
      iii. Margin
      iv. Product mix
      v. Average selling price
B. Setting Quarterly Segment Initiatives
   a. Description
   b. Examples
      i. Lead industry in launch penetration of new system
      ii. Double new account sales within targeted accounts (current quarter vs. prior quarter)
      iii. Increase the number of accounts that have more than one product line installed

iv. Successfully implement new volume discount pricing structure

C. Incentives and Rewards Programs

a. Description

b. Examples

i. Purpose

ii. Description

iii. Who is eligible to participate

iv. Available incentive dollars

v. Rules and length of the incentive program

vi. How will the incentive program be measured

D. Defining Expectations

a. Description

b. Examples

i. Complete a minimum number of outbound sales calls per day

ii. 100 percent compliance on weekly tracking of marketing program executions

iii. Forecasts to be completed and turned in on time to sales manager

Section Two: Segment Marketing Plays

When implementing your segment marketing plays, your play book should include the following information for all of your individual programs:

A. Executive Overview of How Each Individual Play Works

1. *Segment Marketing Coordinator*—Name, telephone, and e-mail address
2. *Description of the Play*—Overview of the strategy and components associated with the play.

3. *Purpose*—What goal are you trying to accomplish with this play?
4. *Value Segment Ranking*—What quadrant within your Value Segment Matrix is this play targeted for?
5. *Decision Maker*—Who are you trying to reach within your customer and prospects' accounts?
6. *Objective*—What specific outcome are you trying to accomplish with this play?
7. *Roles and Responsibilities* —A description of each participant's activities and timelines
8. *Executional Lead Time*—How much time must you allow to actually execute this play?
9. *Diagram*—How the play is to be run
10. *Play Materials*—Presentation materials, scripts, mail pieces
11. *Follow-Up Correspondence*—Letters, e-mails, and proposals
12. *Program Execution Tracking Form*—A review
13. *Nomination Forms*—A review

A. Preparing Customer-Focused Marketing Plays
   a. Conquest—$ segment play
   b. Grow—$$ segment play
   c. Own—$$$ segment play

B. Preparing Product Marketing Plays
   a. Product 1 play
   b. Product 2 play
   c. Product 3 play

C. Preparing Event Marketing Plays
   a. Purpose: "One on many" marketing opportunities designed to establish us as a relevant vendor to mid-mar-

ket companies by demonstrating how our products and services resolve key business issues within their organization

- b. Menu of available event marketing plays
  - i. Trade shows
  - ii. VIP briefings
  - iii. Product demonstrations

D. Preparing Web Marketing Plays

- a. Purpose: Provide customers and prospects with a "self-paced" opportunity to research our products and services
- b. Menu of available Web plays
  - i. Segment specific Web pages
  - ii. Product specific Web pages
  - iii. Specific "play" page incorporated from the individual marketing play
  - iv. Customer specific premier sites

E. Preparing Collateral Marketing Plays

- a. Product data sheets
- b. Product line brochures
- c. Product family brochures
- d. Corporate brochure
- e. Presentation folders and mailing envelopes
- f. Color samples of each of the above collateral materials

Section Three: Product Marketing Support Materials:

A. Purpose

B. Menu of Available Product Marketing Support Materials

- a. Cover letter from product VP describing logic associated with the play
- b. Script for product presentation under nondisclosure

c. Product competitive strengths and weaknesses worksheet

d. Product roadmap with speaker notes

e. Person to call to get internal help with any issue on notebooks

Section Four: Services Marketing Programs

A. Purpose

B. Menu of Available Service Marketing Programs

a. Product overviews and descriptions

b. Suggested services menu

c. Services competitive strengths and weaknesses worksheet

d. Pricing structure

Section Five: Corporate Marketing Sales Support

A. Purpose: Drive Awareness, Consideration, and Purchasing Decision by Establishing Our Brand Among Midsized Companies

B. Menu of Available Corporate Marketing—Sales Support Programs

a. Advertising: Television schedule, print schedule, and copies of ads

b. Corporate Web site

c. Public relations: List of awards won, reprints of favorable articles, Wall Street success, and so on

Section Six: Structured Selling Tools

A. Purpose: Identify, Attract, Develop, and Own High Lifetime Value Customers

a. Understand target needs

b. Identify and document key business issues

c. Approach targets in professional and relevant fashion
d. Presenting company as a resource for resolving issues

B. Structured Selling Tools
a. Color copy of corporate presentation
b. Account planning document
c. Structured selling questions workbook
d. Account planning tactical worksheet
e. Sales opportunity tracking form
f. List of referral customers

Why implement a marketing play book? There are at least two advantages to employing a marketing play:

1. Marketing and sales present a cohesive, coordinated message to appropriate audiences at appropriate times.
2. Keeping free-spirited salespeople from executing their own plays—which may be too expensive and not effective enough—will keep the entire campaign from ending up in a money-losing position.

A good marketing play book is founded on clear documentation, crisp communication, and intense practice. When it is done right, the required actions will be carried out without difficulty or objection by the sales and marketing people charged with executing the plays.

Develop Work Plans

Behind the marketing play is a series of work plans. Carrying out these work plans begins with gathering data and segmenting the market and ends with delivering fresh, accurate, and complete lead reports and marketing tools to well-prepared salespeople. The work plans will map out all deliverables such as creative copy and lead reports and clearly communicate them to the organization.

Using good project management skills and tools is key. Microsoft Project software is a useful tool to use to plan and manage all the tasks associated with execution. You have to plan your people resources and determine linked and sequential activities and back your way to a start date that allows the team to execute flawlessly.

Marketing Vehicles

The initial step in any marketing campaign involves three major activities:

1. Gathering sales and marketing input,
2. Gathering and verifying the required contents and capabilities of your database, and
3. Pulling the data and enhancing it where necessary.

At this point, you have your database.

Step two is to segment customers and prospects by their value to you, and then to identify and target these sites. This is the job for which the Value Segmentation Matrix bears fruit. These first two steps have been covered earlier.

After you have targeted customers and prospects, it's time to decide how you will reach them with your message. This is your marketing vehicle's work plan. The vehicles you employ may range from high-end direct mail to Web activities. The marketing vehicle's work plan is intended to make sure you select the proper vehicles for reaching your target audience and achieving the desired reaction. Some of the marketing vehicles that you may use are:

- Advertising,
- Public relations,

- Personal selling, or
- Sales promotions.

Traditional advertising is the marketing vehicle businesspeople use most of the time to try to accomplish their business aims. Although this book is primarily about direct marketing, traditional advertising has a role to play in the Direct Impact Growth System as well. Conventional print, broadcast and outdoor ads, in both targeted and mass media, can serve to increase awareness of your company or product in advance of more narrowly focused marketing programs using direct mail, e-mail, and other direct means. Corporate Web sites provide another vehicle for delivering marketing campaigns.

Public relations is another very effective marketing tool for many companies. You don't have to pay by the column inch for exposure in magazine and newspaper articles or for airtime on broadcast shows when your company or product is newsworthy. This doesn't mean public relations is free—you pay to have press releases distributed to news outlets and you may have travel and sample expenses as well as the cost of the time you have to spend with media people preparing the coverage. But it's far less expensive than paying for comparable advertising space. And you don't have to hire a public relations firm for a monthly retainer to make use of this vehicle. You can, for instance, list on your Web site any awards your products have won. You can provide references or even active links to favorable articles about your company and products that have appeared in the press.

One of the most attractive features of public relations is its effectiveness. A recommendation in an article or broadcast is generally seen by customers and prospects as unbiased and far more reliable than an advertisement making the same claim. The combination of low cost and strong influence make public relations a useful addition to any marketer's toolkit.

Direct mail is, of course, the direct marketing standby. It is far older as a marketing method than broadcast, online, and telephone marketing, but it remains effective. One advantage of direct mail over media is that you can precisely control who receives your message, as opposed to broadcasting it when who-knows-who is listening or watching. Another very important advantage is that direct mail is trackable. By coding direct mail pieces, you can precisely determine the effectiveness of a given campaign, and repeat it or modify it as indicated.

Many firms have a range of other marketing alternatives as well. Trade shows, public demonstrations, and contests can be effective aids to get your message out, show off your products, and identify and attract interested prospects.

Creative Execution

How important is the copy component of a marketing effort? Direct response creative expert Kim Carpenter says that while lists, media, and offers are proven more important than the creative, the influence of the creative is significant. For instance, she cites a story related by pioneering direct marketer John Caples about how a car repair company increased response by 20 percent simply by changing one word in a headline, from "How to Repair Cars" to "How to Fix Cars" ("How to Evaluate Direct Response Creative," Kim Carpenter & Associates, 2000). In addition, she notes, something as subtle as changing the paper stock has been known to increase response by 8 to 24 percent. And moving from black-and-white to full color printing can increase the response by more than half.

With the help of experiences like those cited, some rules of what makes good creative copy have been formulated. Evaluating creative copy can't, however, be done strictly by numbers. It is a qualitative or even intuitive process sometimes. Furthermore, different media have different needs—what works in telemarketing or online may not work in direct mail or direct response advertising.

However, with those limitations in mind, here are Kim Carpenter's guidelines for good creative copy:

1. Copy should state clearly what it is that you want the audience to do. Remember: Direct marketing is out to generate specific behaviors. You must describe this behavior and provide clear instructions on how to accomplish it, whether it is filling out a Web-based form to request more information or calling a toll-free number to schedule a sales call or product demonstration. If you have more than one action in mind, prioritize them. For instance, you may want targets to return order forms immediately and have requesting more information as a fallback action.
2. Copy that is too clever can sometimes get in the way of generating the desired behavior. Prospects should, for instance, remember the product and the company rather than the ad. Don't let the creative overwhelm the message.
3. The message must be relevant to readers. Any good creative will reflect understanding about what readers:
   - Believe and feel,
   - Want and don't want,
   - Are afraid of and attracted to,
   - How old and educated and wealthy or poor they are,
   - Whether they respond to mailings or ads, and
   - What their job responsibilities are.
4. Creative should appeal to the target audience's:
   - Need to succeed,
   - Need to be the best,
   - Need for recognition,
   - Need not to waste time,
   - Desire to make the right decision,
   - Desire to get a good deal, and
   - Desire not to miss a good opportunity.

5. Good creative should pass the skepticism rule. Read it as if you were a very skeptical person and look for language suggesting there may be a catch and claims that may seem too good to be true.
6. Bear in mind that copy that is true may not seem believable. Make sure your creative is both true and credible.

Setting Schedules

Single-shot marketing promotions are usually not as effective as campaigns calling for multiple exposures, especially when it comes to big-ticket items or business-to-business marketing. The accepted rule of thumb is that it takes seven exposures to a message before it registers with the target audience. Therefore, you should plan to expose your targets to your marketing multiple times before generating the desired behavior. To get the most benefit from your marketing, you have to have a coordinated schedule for making sure your marketing efforts are timed to reinforce each other.

A simple marketing schedule incorporating print advertising, direct mail, and radio spots in a reinforcing and coordinated manner is shown in Figure 7.2. It takes place over a week and is aimed at an audience that consumes local business news and listens to local stations during the morning and evening commutes. The first of three drops in the direct mail schedule is timed to arrive as the first ads are appearing, with the next two arriving as the mass media campaign ends one week later. Coordinating these mail and advertising efforts with outbound telemarketing and sales calls will magnify your message within a relatively short timeframe, and increase the odds of achieving the desired behavior.

This advertising schedule involves more than simple repetition. The print ads, for example, used several different complementary messages that each carried a specific message but which stood on

Figure 7.2 Integrated Marketing Campaign Activities Schedule

	Day 1	Day 2	Day 3	Day 4	Day 5	Day 6	Day 7
Print Advertisements							
• National - Daily	Quarter page	Quarter page	Quarter page		Quarter page	Quarter page	Quarter page
• Metro - Biz Section	Full page		Full page		Quarter page		Full page
• Metro - Daily		Half page		Half page		Half page	
• Magazine - Weekly	Full page						
Radio Advertisements							
• WKRK		AM drive time	AM drive time	AM drive time	AM drive time	AM drive time	
• WZDT		PM drive time	PM drive time	PM drive time	PM drive time	PM drive time	
Direct Mail	To optimize sales follow-up, the direct mail campaign for each audience will be sent out in three waves, each scheduled a day apart from one another.						
• Strategic Accounts	Wave 1a		Wave 2a		Wave 3a		
• High Value Prospects		Wave 1b		Wave 2b		Wave 3b	

its own. But, when seen in the context of the other messages, each message amplified the overall benefits of the offer. In addition to reinforcing the general message, this stair-step approach helped the campaign maintain freshness among those in the target audience who were exposed to the ads several times.

Telemarketing: The 1–2 Punch

Outbound telephone marketing is not just about sales, although telemarketing is an important part of selling in many direct marketing programs. It plays a role in helping you qualify leads generated by calls to information lines, reader response cards, visits to showrooms as well as your advertising and direct mail campaigns. The precise type of information you'll use to qualify leads will vary depending on the product or service you are offering. Business-to-business marketers typically ask responders to confirm their company name, industry, job title, and responsibilities for purchasing products or services. Additional information may include the share of installed products at this site represented by your products (share of wallet), budget, and future purchasing plans. Consumer marketers may ask whether a household consumes the product or service being offered, or whether they are satisfied with their current provider.

Some information may be difficult to gather so settle for logical proxies where you can. Instead of asking what their budget is, you might want to ask about how many products they have and how many they are planning to buy. Applying your current average selling price to this consolidated number, you can approximate their budget without having to probe a sensitive subject. Alternatively, you may be able to obtain much of this information from third-party market research firms.

The information you gather as you talk to your customers and prospects should be entered into your Market Development System and provided to your outbound telemarketers. Armed with accurate data and recent insight into the respondents' needs, your outbound telemarketing representatives can more effectively persuade the target to engage in the desired behavior you want them to pursue.

Lead Reports

The information about qualified leads is ammunition for your salesforce. It isn't doing any good sitting in your marketing database—it has to be in the salesforce's hands for them to be able to use it to reach and influence your target audience. Now is the time for the payoff from your work to create a marketing database that will generate the reports you need. These lead reports must be delivered to the salesforce.

To be truly useful, a lead report has to contain far more than a name and a phone number. It should let the salesperson know what type of organization and individual is being dealt with, the usage and demand for the products you provide, and your current share of this site's budget. A well-rounded lead report will contain this and far more as well. Here are the contents of a typical lead report, with accompanying sales-specific information to help assign and prioritize the call (Figure 7.3 on pp. 184–185):

- Region
- Territory
- Site identifier number
- Number of employees
- Industry
- Company name
- Address
- Phone number
- Budget
- Fiscal year
- Product information (number and type of units)

- Share of wallet by product
- Contact name
- Contact title
- Function
- Address
- Phone
- Other phone
- Fax
- E-mail address
- Date first contacted
- Date last contacted
- Appointment scheduled
- Next contact
- Notes
- Salesperson

You should have much of this information in your Marketing Development System database—previously gathered from your own records and supplemented by outside sources. Telemarketing lead-qualification calls will supply much of the rest. It's not essential that every blank be filled in. You may not know the budget and installed units plans for every customer and prospect. But a spreadsheet containing entries for these categories should be mostly full.

Your sales team is a rich source of this type of information, and providing them with a summarized view of their territory will encourage them to provide you with any missing information that you are looking for. Chances are they have never had this type of support before. When they are exposed to the database and taught to use it appropriately, it will reinforce their desire and commitment to getting and maintaining data in the database. This in turn will make the database more powerful.

Figure 7.3 Territory Management Reports

Region	Terr	Value Segment Quad	Siteid	# of Emp	SIC	Company	Primary Address
SE	VIR	3	114747149	1500	4813	AT&T	3033 CHAIN BRIDGE RD RM B120
SE	VIR	3	109778445	1200	6022	CRESTAR BANK OPERATIONS CENTER	1001 SEMMES AVE
SE	VIR	3	109778699	1200	7374	G E FANUC AUTOMATIONINC	RTE 29 N AND RTE 606
SE	VIR	3	114760234	2000	3625	GE INDUSTRIAL CONTROL SYSTEMS	1501 ROANOKE BLVD RM 215
SE	VIR	3	108830683	700	481302	GTE FEDERAL SYSTEMS	15000 CONFERENCE CENTER DR
SE	VIR	3	108717783	1500	602101	NATIONSBANK	8001 VILLA PARK DR
SE	VIR	3	109008295	1000	381201	ORBITAL SCIENCES CORP	21700 ATLANTICBLVD
SE	VIR	3	108726744	1760	873101	RAYTHEON SYSTEMS CO	7700 ARLINGTON BLVD
SE	VIR	3	112867416	1100	7373	T R W FEDERAL SYSTEMS GROUP	12900 FEDERAL SYSTEMS DR
SE	VIR	3	114726527	700	8731	TASC	12100 SUNSET HILLS RD STE

Territory Management Report contains:

- Region
- Territory
- Site identifier
- Number of employees
- Industry codes
- Address
- Phone number
- Contact dates
- Budget
- Fiscal year end

Sales Lead -

Terr	Site Id	Site Contact Ic	Company Name	Title	First Name	Last Name	Job Title Code	
VIR	114747149	1147471490004	AT&T	MR	LEO	ROCHE	PROJECT MANAGER	DIR
VIR	109778445	1097784450011	CRESTAR BANK OPERATIONS CENTER	MR	JAMES	WILSON	EXECUTIVE VP/DIRECTOR OF HR	PER
VIR	109778699	1097786990009	G E FANUC AUTOMATION INC	MR	DONALD	BORWHAT	VP OF EMPLOYEE RELATIONS	PER
VIR	114760234	1147602340002	GE INDUSTRIAL CONTROL SYSTEMS	MR	THOMAS	BROCK	VP/GENERAL MANAGER	CEO
VIR	108830683	1088306830009	GTE FEDERAL SYSTEMS	MS	SUSAN	DUFF	DIRECTOR OF HUMAN RESOURCES	PER
VIR	108717783	1087177830002	NATIONSBANK	MS	DENISE	RIMES	HUMAN RESOURCE DIRECTOR	PER
VIR	109008295	1090082950008	ORBITAL SCIENCES CORP	MR	MICHAEL	KEEGAN	CONTROLLER	CON
VIR	108726744	1087267440003	RAYTHEON SYSTEMS CO	MR	KENNETH	YANCY	VP OF HUMAN RESOURCES	PER
VIR	112867416	1128674160001	T R W FEDERAL SYSTEMS GROUP	MR	ROBERT	WATERS	VP HUMAN RESOURCE	PER
VIR	114726527	1147265270002	TASC	MR	ANTHONY	BORGHI	DIRECTOR OF PERSONNEL	PER

Site Contact Report contains:

- Contact name
- Contact title
- Functional responsibilities
- Address
- Phone
- Fax
- E-mail
- Contact dates
- Notes
- Sales reps name

City	ST	ZIP	ZIP4	Phone#	Fiscal Year End	Estimated Budget	Product # 1			
							Total Prod # 1(like) Installed	Top Prod # 1(like) Competitor	% Top Prod # 1(like) Comp	Your Total Prod # 1 Installed
OAKTON	VA	22124	2542	(703) 6915000	03	1019666	1500	Capital Solutions	75.0	0
RICHMOND	VA	23224	2245	(804) 7825000	03	1186999	1537	Oakmount Supplies	64.3	0
CHARLOTTESVILLE	VA	22901		(804) 9785000	03	1084333	896	Tryton Analytics	89.8	0
SALEM	VA	24153	6422	(540) 3877200	03	1653333	1500	Delta Services	26.7	10
CHANTILLY	VA	20151	3819	(703) 8184000	03	1045333	1163	Delta Services	94.6	0
RICHMOND	VA	23228	6501	(804) 6434013	03	2491666	1275	Alpha Systems	80.0	9
STERLING	VA	20166	6801	(703) 4065000	03	1473666	880	Medbiz Technology	50.0	24
FALLS CHURCH	VA	22042	2902	(703) 5605000	03	1579666	1859	Tryton Analytics	80.0	0
FAIRFAX	VA	22033		(703) 9681000	03	1110333	1500	Delta Services	35.0	0
RESTON	VA	20190	3233	(703) 8345000	03	1143666	205	Capital Solutions	80.5	5

- Product / services information
  - > Total number installed
  - > Top competitor
  - > Total number of your products installed
- Share of wallet by product

Site Contact Report

Primary Street Address	City	State	ZIP	Zip4	Telephone Number (main)	Telephone Number (direct)	Fax	Email Address	Date Followed Up	Date For Scheduled Appointment
3033 CHAIN BRIDGE RD RM B120	OAKTON	VA	22124	2542	(703) 6915000					
1001 SEMMES AVE	RICHMOND	VA	23224	2245	(804) 7825000					
RTE 29 N AND RTE 606	CHARLOTTESVILLE	VA	22901		(804) 9785000					
1501 ROANOKE BLVD RM 215	SALEM	VA	24153	6422	(540) 3877200					
15000 CONFERENCE CENTER DR	CHANTILLY	VA	20151	3819	(703) 8184000					
8001 VILLA PARK DR	RICHMOND	VA	23228	6501	(804) 6434013					
21700 ATLANTIC BLVD	STERLING	VA	20166	6801	(703) 4065000		(703) 4063502			
7700 ARLINGTON BLVD	FALLS CHURCH	VA	22042	2902	(703) 5605000					
12900 FEDERAL SYSTEMS DR	FAIRFAX	VA	22033		(703) 9681000					
12100 SUNSET HILLS RD STE	RESTON	VA	20190	3233	(703) 8345000					

Communicating the Plan

One of the primary purposes of marketing work plans is to communicate the organization's marketing objectives, the means that are being employed to reach them and the status of the efforts to accomplish those goals. It is marketing's responsibility to see that work plans are created and disseminated in a timely manner and in a format that will facilitate this communication. Weekly or more frequent status meetings should be held to update marketing and other personnel on the progress of the marketing campaign. At Direct Impact, when we are in peak execution mode, we hold daily sales and marketing meetings. Providing shared access to schedules helps everyone get information when they need it, and keeps the entire program on track.

Facts to Remember

- A well-executed marketing play is the end result of carrying out a series of work plans that begins with gathering data and segmenting the market and ends with delivering fresh, accurate, and complete lead reports and marketing tools to well-prepared salespeople.
- The marketing vehicles work plan is intended to make sure you select the proper vehicles for reaching your target audience and achieving the desired reaction.
- Although this book is primarily about direct marketing, traditional advertising has a role to play in the Direct Impact System as well. Conventional print, broadcast, and outdoor ads, in both targeted and mass media, can serve to increase awareness of your company or product in advance of more narrowly focused marketing using direct mail, e-mail, and other direct means. Corporate Web

sites provide another vehicle for delivering marketing campaigns.

- Creativity is often considered synonymous with a free-flowing inventiveness. But, paradoxically, the best creative is generated when constraints are applied. Great creatives are developed from a tight creative brief.
- To get the most benefit from the required several exposures to your marketing you have to have a coordinated schedule for making sure your marketing efforts are timed to reinforce each other.
- Outbound telephone marketing has a place in many direct marketing campaigns as a tool for qualifying leads generated by calls to information lines, reader response cards, visits to showrooms, and advertising and direct mail campaigns.
- The information about qualified leads is ammunition for your salesforce. It isn't doing any good sitting in your marketing database—it has to be in the salesforce's hands for them to be able to use it to reach and influence your target audience. Now is the time for the payoff from your work to create a marketing database that will generate the reports you need. These lead reports must now be delivered to the salesforce.
- One of the primary purposes of marketing work plans is to communicate the organization's marketing objectives, the means that are being employed to reach them and the status of the efforts to accomplish those goals. It is marketing's responsibility to see that work plans are created and disseminated in a timely manner and in a format that will facilitate this communication.

STEP

8

Sales Execution

One of the traditions of Hartford, Connecticut, is an event known as the Charter Oak Affair. In 1687, the overbearing British governor of New England, Sir Edmund Andros, demanded the colonists surrender the royal charter establishing the Connecticut colony so he could put into action King James II's plan for consolidating all the colonies into one. They wouldn't give it up, so Andros went to Hartford to look for the document. When he got there, he still couldn't find it because, the story has it, Captain John Wadsworth had hidden it in a giant oak tree growing in downtown Hartford. The royal repeal of the colony's charter was short-lived and the document was reinstated as the basis of Connecticut law just a few years later following a shift of power in England. The Charter Oak Affair symbolizes the Americans' substitution of respect for constitutional rights to allegiance to the King of England.

If you've spent time working in marketing or sales, you may find elements of this story strangely familiar. Consider Andros to be a caricature of a high-handed and theoretical marketer. Wadsworth fills the role of an archetypal salesperson: individualistic, free-spirited, and resentful of interference from marketers seemingly removed from practical concerns. Throw in the possibility that the salesperson may hide vital information from marketing and the resemblance becomes positively eerie.

Maybe this is news to you, but the fact is, in many of the companies we've spent time with, similar oppression, underground terrorism, and even active warfare has been waged between factions of the same company, namely, sales versus marketing. Depending on what side of the fence you are sitting on, you might recognize yourself in either Captain Wadsworth or Sir Andros. But whatever your personal sympathies are, such internecine warfare benefits no one, least of all the health of the company harboring the combatants. As Abraham Lincoln paraphrased St. Mark, "A house divided against itself cannot stand." It's important to get sales and marketing smoothly working together if you expect your own house to stand.

A story of one brief engagement—also in Hartford—with one of our clients illustrates the antagonism between sales and marketing and the efforts one marketing executive put forth to resolve and defuse the bitterness between the two departments. The company was struggling. Sales were not arriving at the rate required. Marketing had gone through a series of destabilizing transitions and a new vice president of marketing had recently been installed to help the company reestablish itself in the professional services market. Through the transition period, sales had not seen anything of note from the marketing department. The sales team had developed the attitude that marketing wasn't going to be able to come up with anything meaningful so they were determined to slug through it alone. They would carry the weight and find the big orders needed to deliver the numbers—a real bunch of martyrs.

The marketing vice president had called a meeting to try to present some information to the sales vice president that would convince him that marketing had something to offer—like Governor Andros, she hoped to drag the essential document out of the oak tree. The new vice president of marketing had done her homework after coming on board and had analyzed the company's performance over the last two quarters. She noticed that the sales department was closing some business, but the deals were far smaller than the big orders the situation called for. In addition, these new accounts did not convert to long-term clients once the initial professional engagement was completed. These conversions and their associated additional revenues were key components of the company's business strategy, but they weren't occurring as often as necessary to fuel the company's revenue growth.

The vice president of marketing wasn't naive and she knew that marketing's thrashing over the last several quarters clearly had contributed to the uphill battle sales was fighting. She knew that she was being brought in to solve marketing's executional failures but, equally important, she knew that she needed to reach out to and engage the sales department for the company as a whole to be successful. Without sales' genuine commitment and involvement, she wasn't going to be successful.

She called a meeting, with us there to look on, and presented her analysis of the company's performance, the marketing opportunity, and marketing's objectives. We had set up an integrated sales and marketing pro forma that contained all of her analysis. Projecting this spreadsheet on the conference room screen, she invited the sales vice president to debate her assumptions. Working interactively with specific outcomes shown on the screen as every assumption was revised, the sales vice president quickly came to realize that going it alone meant going nowhere. Unless the sales department was able to dramatically increase its close rates, move up into larger accounts, and convert initial purchasers into long-term contracts, the company was not going to survive.

By presenting factual financial numbers in a meaningful business exercise, we were able to bring the two warring factions together and forge a working team. Once the sales vice president saw the crisis his team was heading for, he was much more receptive to understanding and installing a more disciplined approach to selling in his sales team.

One of the principles of a relationship marketing environment is that marketing acts in support of sales, not in spite of sales.

This anecdote is not presented as evidence of marketing's superiority to sales in the Direct Impact Growth System nor to position marketing as managing sales. The salespeople in this example clearly needed help in achieving their goals. Marketing is often in a position to help by providing information and processes that can assist the sales team proactively approach profitable accounts. As marketing puts the proper market intelligence information in place, the sales department's task is to implement an approach that extracts and maximizes the value of each customer and prospect. Similarly, marketing must work cooperatively with sales to gather market information, determine what support needs are required, and tailor the tools to the task.

The manner in which sales works in the Direct Impact Growth System is called *Structured Selling*. Making this happen, from the sales team's perspective, is a matter of sales execution.

Structured Selling

Structured Selling is a system for boosting sales results by implementing five major components—account planning, marketing programs, sales calls, ongoing interaction, and performance measurement.

At first glance, the term Structured Selling may call to mind a mechanical, sell-by-the-numbers approach (Figure 8.1). Or it may suggest a narrow, our-way-or-the-highway philosophy of selling. Neither of these concepts is correct. It is not an attempt to force a particular methodology on a sales team. Rather, it simply provides

Figure 8.1 Structured Selling

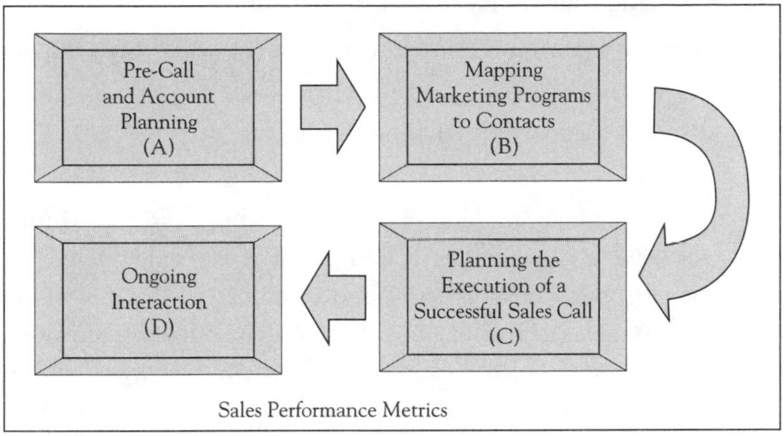

Pre-Call and Account Planning (A)

Mapping Marketing Programs to Contacts (B)

Planning the Execution of a Successful Sales Call (C)

Ongoing Interaction (D)

Sales Performance Metrics

the framework for an integrated, closed-loop sales and marketing effort. The sales methodology employed with it is up to you.

Structured Selling consists of two closely linked areas: Planning and Execution. Each area has two key components. Planning includes Account Planning and Marketing Programs. Execution contains Sales Calls and Ongoing Interaction.

Account Planning

The first part of Structured Selling is *Account Planning*—examining *your* knowledge of your accounts. Properly implemented, Structured Selling asks a series of questions ideally tailored to your specific environment and sales team's maturity, to ensure that your sales and marketing teams have a clear and accurate understanding of your strategic accounts, and the opportunities within. Structured Selling revolves around four primary considerations:

1. Understanding your business opportunity,
2. Assessing your ability to win the account,
3. Determining what return on investment you should expect, and
4. Deciding how to approach an account.

The first component, understanding your business opportunity, involves knowing the customer's budget for your products and services, the customer's buying plans, and your current share of wallet. Your understanding of the account should include its organizational structure; corporate objectives; present financial performance; important events such as mergers, competitive threats, or layoffs. Most if not all of this information should already be included in your Market Development System database. Extracting and analyzing it will give you the ability to categorize and rank customers and prospects based on the business opportunity they represent. This knowledge will guide your sales targets and approaches.

Assess your ability to win the account by evaluating your products and services in terms of customer needs and competitive offerings. You will need to have an idea of your image in the marketplace and how customers view you and your products. You'll have to have good information about your competitors' positions in your current and prospective accounts. Also consider your future product plans and, as far as you can determine, your competitors' initiatives and responses.

Determining what return on investment you should expect requires estimating the amount of effort, dollars, and other resources it will take to generate a given number of sales in any account. This calculation will yield different returns depending on the opportunity represented by the customer, by your ability to win the business, and on the particular buying process each account exhibits. You rank accounts by projected return and make your decision about which ones to pursue, in what order, by matching the projected returns against your corporate goals.

Deciding how to approach an account is a matter of identifying decision makers and assessing decision-making processes, budget cycles, and budget timeframes. You should already be sure that the account has a need for what you are selling. At the same time, you must take into consideration the salesperson's relationships with decision makers and influencers. The end result is a plan for contacting, informing, and selling to each account. Selecting an approach will build on the three previous elements. Without knowing your business opportunity, your chances of success, and your likely return on investment, you can't decide intelligently how to affordably and appropriately approach an account. Once you've determined your targets and verified their profitability, you are now able to select the marketing plays you want to use to gain access to these decision makers and accelerate your relationships.

Winning Over the Sales Team

Account and territory planning is sometimes viewed as sheer punishment or torture by the sales team. Of course, planning activities are not meant to be that way at all. Account and territory planning is and should be a fundamental cornerstone of your sales activities. Good account and territory planning provides an outstanding integration touch-point between and sales and marketing. Properly presented account plans identify specific marketing programs the sales representatives wish to deploy within their territories, reinforcing your marketing teams understanding of sales' needs and sales' understanding of the programs that you have put into place.

Most sales representatives dislike the idea of territory and account planning and often come up with a variety of reasons why they can't do it. Typically, they say that it takes too long and they can't find the information that management is looking for. With the advent of the Internet, a variety of information and information resources are readily available to your sales teams making it easier to gather relevant and pertinent information about their territories. Furthermore, once this information has been gathered and input into your Market Development System database, it will be even more accessible.

Continuous communication between sales and marketing cannot be overlooked. Sales must understand how marketing programs can be executed and, importantly, how they will be measured before sales efforts can be integrated effectively with marketing. Account planning is an ongoing exercise. At a minimum, there should be regular account reviews. Adjustments to strategies and tactics should be discussed, documented, and implemented in the sales and marketing departments as needs are identified.

Marketing Programs

As a practical matter, the majority of the responsibility for sales execution naturally rests with the sales management and sales personnel. But marketing has a very important role to play. It is marketing's responsibility to develop marketing plays and campaigns that are relevant to the sales team's needs. Marketing and sales work together as do players on a sports team to execute marketing plays. These marketing plays must be completed and articulated with all costs identified prior to the sales team's account planning and territory planning assignments. Marketing and sales jointly decide which customers to go after, basing their decisions on marketing research, their territory's Value Segmentation Matrix, and their documented account plans. Sales can't call a play and decide who to run these plays against unless they clearly understand every aspect of the play and its execution. This close-knit coordination is required for sales and marketing programs to yield their true potential.

Marketing prepares the sales department by educating them about the campaign plan, prepares the market with direct mail and other vehicles, and guides the sales team in approaching customers and prospects in a manner calculated to yield optimum results consistent with corporate objectives. This coordination reaches its ultimate in a marketing play. A series of marketing plays is a campaign.

Marketing plays start with specific objectives. These objectives may be customer-focused, aimed at particular spaces on the Customer Relationship Continuum. Or they may be product-focused, designed to affect the sales of specific products.

For instance, a marketing play may be aimed at customers who are buying little or nothing from you at the moment, with the objective of identifying the most promising members of that group and turning them into grow-level customers.

For example, a product-focused play may be intended to increase sales of notebook computers, or leverage off the company's planned introduction of a new server line.

Salespeople's activity in marketing plays begins by understanding all of the marketing materials that will be circulated to target customers. These materials may consist of direct mail letters, e-mail newsletters, television ads, demonstration videos, and so on. They may also include telemarketing scripts, answers to objections, and other sales support materials that customers don't see.

Salespeople need to understand and consistently reinforce the marketing messages that customers and prospects are receiving from your company through its marketing campaign. Marketing also supports sales by providing specific sales support materials. These may consist of product overviews and descriptions, suggested specific configurations or services that a customer may be offered, competitive matrices, and pricing structures. Marketing also provides sales tools such as compilations of awards that your company has won, favorable articles, and the like.

The essence of the marketing programs' role in Structured Selling is to coordinate with and boost sales' efforts and success rates. Marketing's job is to set the table and send out the invitations. Sales is expected to bring the guests home. And the feast, consisting of your goods and services, should be so appealing that your customers want to come back for more.

Sales Calls

Executing successful sale calls in targeted accounts is what it all comes down to and this is the objective of Structured Selling.

Whatever your specific sales methodology, its purpose is going to be to identify, attract, develop, and own high lifetime value customers. The Structured Selling technique increases your chances at each stage of this process, none more so than when you are actually in front of a customer making your sales presentation.

A successful sales call can be viewed as consisting of five steps or sections:

1. Greet
2. Qualify
3. Demonstrate
4. Present
5. Close

- *Greet.* The first step in a successful sales call is to approach your target customer in a professional and relevant fashion. The definition of professionalism varies—you wouldn't project the same image if you were selling pest control services to corporations as you would if you were selling financial services to individuals. Match your image and approach to your market and, above all, see that the image you project is relevant to your target customer.
- *Qualify.* Make sure you are calling on the right person, at the right company to make the most of your valuable time and energy. Ascertain that your target is, indeed, the decision maker or influencer you had indicated in your database. Also see that you understand the business or other special needs of your target customer. Identify key discontinuity issues that are currently troubling your customers. For instance, a manufacturing business

may be struggling with new labeling requirements demanded by its customers. A consumer may be having trouble finding a product that meets the household budget and health requirements as his or her family expands and matures. Recall the axiom that sales representatives have two ears and only one mouth—listen far more than you speak. As you hear the customer propound on problems, take notes. These will become the foundation of your demonstration, presentation, and close. They also get fed back into the database.

- *Demonstrate.* You need to show the prospect or customer the features and the benefits of what you are offering. This may involve anything from showing a sample of your product to actually demonstrating a device you are offering. The idea is to familiarize your prospect with the valuable results your product or service can provide.
- *Present.* Now put forth your company, your products, and services as a solution. Don't take on the whole load yourself, however. Get your customers to assess and, if possible, express the value of being able to solve the problems he or she faces. Once they articulate the vision of their solution, it's time move to the final step.
- *Close.* This is the part where you ask for the order, request the signature on the contract, or otherwise formalize the sale of your goods or services to the prospect. This final act is preceded by important details including finalizing the amount of goods and products being ordered, their delivery date, any special pricing or financing, and so on. Beyond obtaining this order, your goal should be to position yourself as a valuable extension of and resource to your customers. This is the type of trust-based relationship that spurs long-term, high-profit business relationships.

Having a concise set of steps for sales representatives to follow helps keep your sales representatives on track. Clearly understanding what has to be done gives the sales representative the confidence to do it.

Confidence, in turn, inspires conviction—a belief in your products and services that your customers can see and understand. That conviction leads to their commitment—first to entertain your proposal, then ultimately to select your product or service as their chosen solution. Closing the account provides your sales team with their commissions and commissions translate into spending cash. Show us a sale representative who isn't interested in a proven, step-by-step approach to making more money and we will show you a sales representative that will never work for us:

- Clarity leads to confidence.
- Confidence leads to conviction.
- Conviction leads to commitment.
- Commitment leads to closure.
- Closure leads to commissions.
- Commissions lead to cash.

In addition to meeting these broad objectives, successful sales calls must be conducted by people equipped with the appropriate Structured Selling tools. In the Direct Impact Growth System (DIGS), salespeople are equipped with more than order pads. To take advantage of the leverage and magnification opportunities presented in the relationship marketing environment, salespeople must fully understand the tools contained within your marketing plays and general sales tool kit. These may include:

- Copies of advertisements or brochures to which the customer may have been exposed.
- Polished presentation materials such as slide shows.
- Account planning materials for review prior to conducting sales calls.

- Workbooks to help sales representatives practice answering questions from prospects.
- Daily activity tracking forms such as call reports.
- Application examples with specific system features, functions, and benefits.
- Testimonials and marquee account lists.
- General corporate backgrounders.

Having these materials prepared helps build the sales representative's confidence. Knowing in advance what questions are likely to be asked by your customers and having answers on hand is a powerful confidence-builder. It also means the representative won't be as tempted to launch into an over-elaborate explanation of the product or service that may answer too many questions while ignoring the one that is most important. Overall, the combination of overarching principles centered on understanding and addressing customer needs, with the tactical tools required for completing successful sales, means the Structured Selling sales team is fully-equipped to increase close rates and bottom-line performance.

Ongoing Interaction

The Direct Impact Growth System is about creating rapid, profitable, sustainable growth—not getting one-time sales with limited profitability and doubtful prospects for long-term relationship-building. That's why ongoing interaction with targeted accounts is a pillar of Structured Selling.

Ongoing interaction involves more than just follow-up communications after the sale. Ongoing interaction actually begins before the sale, in a process that may reach 20 or more steps from gathering initial information about account needs to placing evaluation units or free samples and scheduling ongoing, postsale status reports and meetings. Figure 8.2 is an example of a specific value track of ongoing interactions. Value tracks are often set up as a part of a specific marketing play and outline all of the steps and/or supporting activities associated with the continued communication you wish to have with your accounts. Value tracks are typically tied to the individual quadrants of your Value Segmentation Matrix. The higher the value of the account you are trying to penetrate, the more activities or the higher the quality of the activities you may incorporate within your value track. Figure 8.2 is a visual blueprint of an ongoing interaction plan that you may want to consider.

Each of these items represents a specific activity or opportunity for you to add value to your customer and deepen your relationship. Many promising relationships have been ruined when the sales representative starts behaving as though the job is done when he or she gets the order. In reality, the job has just begun because the sales representative has set a level of expectation in the customer's mind and those expectations must be exceeded. The actions shown in Figure 8.2 illustrate an activity yardstick that can be used to make sure you are executing before, during, and after the sales process. Simple things like introducing additional resources such as technical support, customer service, or training personnel go a long way toward enhancing your relationships. The same is true when your client receives sincere and appropriate correspondence from executives within your company. An invitation to an executive forum or a special event makes the customer feel like he or she is appreciated. A handwritten thank-you note will go a long way toward reinforcing your customer's decision to purchase your product as well. Subtle but sincere interactions provide a personal touch that distinguishes your firm from your competition. It's simple, it's effective, and it's inexpensive to do. Including this type of detail and prepacking some of these communications within your overall value track accelerates execution and increases the ongoing interactions you may have within these accounts.

It's easy to see that this sort of ongoing interaction gives salespeople the best opportunity for crafting long-term relationships

Figure 8.2 Ongoing Interaction

- Ongoing Interaction D
  - Written Correspondence A
    - Post Call Follow-Up Letters/E-mails 1
    - Marketing Follow-Up 1
      - Marketing Program Correspondence 2
        - Low Value Communications Track 3
          - Direct Mail Biz Catalog 4
        - High Value Communications Track 3
          - Valued Customer/Prospect Letters/E-mails 4
          - Product Marketing 5
          - Service and Support 6
          - Financial Services 7
          - Other 8
  - Verbal Correspondence B
    - Sales Follow-Up Telephone Calls 1
  - On-Site Interactions C
    - Fact Finding Visits 1
    - Sales Presentations 2
    - Product Presentations 3
    - Reference Visits 4
    - Executive Briefings 5
    - Cost Justifications 6
    - Formal Proposal 7
    - Status Meetings 8

with customers., What does your customer receive from your company's implementation of Structured Selling? How about:

- A higher appreciation by your client of your skills and individual value to their business,
- Better understanding of your company's capabilities, and
- Keener appreciation of your organization's products and services and more productive sales calls.

Sales and Marketing Execution Measurement

Sales execution is a multifaceted responsibility entailing conducting the required calls and presentations, meeting deadlines, communicating expectations, managing the sales team, and adjusting on-the-fly to react to response levels and other issues that crop up.

While meeting deadlines is always important in sales, in Structured Selling it takes on added significance. If sales efforts are to reinforce marketing campaigns, timing is of paramount importance. Customers and prospects need to be contacted while your marketing messages are fresh in their minds, and salespeople need to know exactly what messages and vehicles their customers and prospects have been exposed to. These considerations require strict adherence to deadlines. It's up to sales management to monitor and enforce compliance with deadlines.

Management of a sales team, whether it has to do with deadlines or other matters, begins with communication. Salespeople must have objectives, targets, timelines, and metrics. They must have the key components of a marketing and sales effort explained to them so that a lack of understanding can't be used as an excuse for failure to execute.

It's of particular importance that metrics—the measures by which sales' performance will be evaluated—be explained in detail. Salespeople need to know what is being measured. It's a good idea to make sure they know that marketing is also being measured. The number of pieces mailed, number of outbound calls, number of Web hits, and other measures will be applied to marketers just as other metrics are applied to sales. Everyone is accountable in a Structured Selling environment. Sales metrics may include the following:

- Number of sites followed up
- Number of outbound calls
- Number of inbound returned calls
- Number of targeted contacts reached
- Average number of calls to reach contact
- Number of new contacts and referrals
- Number of scheduled appointments
- Number of completed presentations
- Appointment rates
- Presentation rates
- Close rates

These measures can and probably will be sorted out by region, territory, play (customer- or product-focused), and salesperson. In addition, sales revenue measures will also be tracked, including:

- Revenues by product,
- Revenues by service, and
- Revenues by value segment

The relationship between metrics and sales incentives must also be crystal clear. Salespeople are best motivated by receiving rewards for achieving identified goals. Depending on your company's philosophy, you may or may not want to establish incentives for every goal your sales team has to hit. Whatever your incentive philosophy is, if incentives are used then incentives have to be paid out in a timely manner. If they are not, your rewards programs are dismissed as meaningless and intangible. When Janet was selling cars, the bonuses were given in cash in the middle of the showroom floor—that was motivation.

Be smart about your incentives. Companies employ a wide variety of sales incentives to motivate their salesforces. Early on at Dell, our incentive programs were a hodge-podge of throwing cash around. It seemed as though our solution to every sales problem we encountered was "spiff it" (spiff = shorthand for a sales incentive) or "throw another contest at the sales reps." It was an accounting headache and often confused rather than motivated the sales. Over time, we found that simpler incentives were not only easier to understand, but more profitable for both individual salespeople and for the company as a whole.

Reinforcing your Organizational Magnification philosophies, goals relating to incentives should be clearly tied to broader corporate objectives. Salespeople are by nature instinctively aware of where they are in relation to hitting their numbers. That's another way of saying that incentives drive performance. Therefore, incentives must be carefully set relative to corporate objectives, measured by transparent methods, and reliably result in the payout of appropriate rewards.

Measurement and Tracking Reports

In Patrick's early days at IBM, he had two sales managers who used what they called *totem pole reporting* to motivate the sales team. Every Wednesday, the previous week's sales performance and year-to-date totals for each salesperson were ranked and posted for all to see. Needless to say, no one liked to see his or her name on the bottom of the totem pole. The weekly posting even spurred side bets on who would be highest. This friendly competition further motivated the sales representatives to adopt the desired behavior and, as a result, it accelerated performance.

Not all measurement is about providing incentives to sales personnel. The measurement and tracking in a Direct Impact Growth System (DIGS) is primarily intended to provide information back into the system so your objectives, techniques, and campaigns can be adjusted to reflect real-world results. By definition therefore, measurement and tracking is a central component of your sales execution activities (Figures 8.3, 8.4, and 8.5).

The information presented earlier—numbers, names, and titles of persons reached on sales calls, the number of calls required to reach targets, the number of appointments confirmed—guides the adjustments you'll make to your overall programs. For instance, if sales finds that a higher-than-expected number of calls is required to reach decision makers, the marketing team will have to feed that information into the pro forma projecting financial outcomes. This may result in an adjusted estimate of bottom-line performance of the campaign. It may call for modifying execution to provide for additional e-mail or other contacts in advance of sales calls to raise awareness and prepare customers and prospects for the call. As always, a keen eye will continually be focused on identifying unresponsive accounts and eliminating subsequent communications to them.

It is sales management's job to measure the sales team's performance. The primary source of the data sales management will use in measurement and tracking will be in the documentation and forms that your salespeople use to complete their daily activities—making calls, setting appointments, conducting presentations, and booking orders. However, other monitoring will also prove productive in increasing the effectiveness of sales execution. This may take the form of sales managers listening in on sales telephone calls to customers and prospects, accompanying salespeople on sales presentations to a spectrum of accounts, or other actions. In either case, attention is paid to whether or not the sales message is being articulated consistently in concert with the marketing message and whether salespeople are effectively leveraging the tools marketing has provided to

Figure 8.3 Sales Performance Metrics—Marketing Plays—Direct Mail

Metro Program	Sales Efficiencies - Direct Mail							
	# of Sites Followed Up	# of Outbound Calls	# of Inbound/ Returned Calls	# of Targeted Contacts Reached	Average # of Calls To Reach Contact	# of New Contact/Referrals	# of Scheduled Appointments	# of Completed Presentations
Chicago								
1 Marketing Play #1								
2 Marketing Play #2								
3 Marketing Play #3								
4 Marketing Play #4								
Minneapolis								
1 Marketing Play #1								
2 Marketing Play #2								
3 Marketing Play #3								
4 Marketing Play #4								
North East Regional Totals								
Boston								
1 Marketing Play #1								
2 Marketing Play #2								
3 Marketing Play #3								
4 Marketing Play #4								
New York								
1 Marketing Play #1								
2 Marketing Play #2								
3 Marketing Play #3								
4 Marketing Play #4								
Northeast Regional Totals								
Campaign Totals								

Figure 8.4 Sales Performance Metrics—Marketing Plays—Web Performance

Metro	Program	Sales Efficiencies - Web Follow Up							
Metro	Program	# of Sites Followed Up	# of Outbound Calls	# of Inbound/ Returned Calls	# of Targeted Contacts Reached	Average # of Calls To Reach Contact	# of New Contact/Referrals	# of Scheduled Appointments	# of Completed Presentations
Chicago									
	1 Marketing Play #1								
	2 Marketing Play #2								
	3 Marketing Play #3								
	4 Marketing Play #4								
Minneapolis									
	1 Marketing Play #1								
	2 Marketing Play #2								
	3 Marketing Play #3								
	4 Marketing Play #4								
Northcentral Regional Totals									
Boston									
	1 Marketing Play #1								
	2 Marketing Play #2								
	3 Marketing Play #3								
	4 Marketing Play #4								
New York									
	1 Marketing Play #1								
	2 Marketing Play #2								
	3 Marketing Play #3								
	4 Marketing Play #4								
Northeast Regional Totals									
	Campaign Totals								

Figure 8.5 Sales Performance Metrics—Marketing Plays—Revenue Performance

		Services Revenues						Product Revenues			
Metro	Program	Services #1	Services #2	Services #3	Services #4	Services #5	Services #6	Product #1	Product #2	Product #3	Totals
Chicago											
	1 Product #1										
	2 Product #2										
	3 Product #3										
	4 Product #4										
Minneapolis											
	1 Product #1										
	2 Product #2										
	3 Product #3										
	4 Product #4										
Northcentral Regional Totals											
Boston											
	1 Product #1										
	2 Product #2										
	3 Product #3										
	4 Product #4										
New York											
	1 Product #1										
	2 Product #2										
	3 Product #3										
	4 Product #4										
Northeast Regional Totals											
	Campaign Totals										

them. In addition, the effectiveness of these marketing tools can be tweaked in the field. Making adjustments to salespeople's calls, presentations, and techniques should be handled with positive coaching and counseling by your sales management team.

Don't stop at explaining how the sales department will be measured. Build a bridge between sales and marketing that explains marketing's mission and how marketing is being measured. Unfortunately, salespeople often think of marketing as nothing more than overhead. To overcome this perception, it's important that sales understand that marketing's role is to provide the "air cover" that supports the "ground assaults" that sales is engaged in. They need to understand that sales is not the only organization accountable for the success or failure of their organization.

This is a good time to present the marketing pro forma to the sales team. A good guess is that a third of the salespeople exposed to marketing's pro forma will grasp its significance and become more aware and vocally appreciative of marketing's role and the challenges the marketing team faces. Their execution will most likely increase. Another third will execute, but won't become marketing advocates. The final third won't care much one way or the other. Don't spend your time trying to endear yourself to this last third. You've got a marketplace to tackle with or without them. It is better to concentrate your efforts on those who "get it" than those that don't.

The goal of presenting sales with marketing's mission and measurements isn't to get sales to appreciate and say wonderful things about marketing. Your goal is to have salespeople execute against the company's objectives. By sharing marketing objectives and how marketing is being measured, you can facilitate this understanding and, for most sales teams, improve execution.

Sales Execution Summary

We would love to say that our marketing and sales executives and teams in Hartford learned to work together, that everyone executed flawlessly and the company grew to become a preeminent player in the professional services space. The reality is that while the two teams did begin to work more closely, questionable management and financial misstatements garnered the company some very damaging coverage in the trade press and the company never was able to recover.

Our point here is that even the best intentions for working together and adhering to the disciplines and principles of Structured Selling and the Direct Impact Growth System, don't always lead to legendary status in the annals of American business. Bad management can undermine the very best of foundations.

Another thing we want to make very clear is that *Planting Flowers, Pulling Weeds* is not just about marketing—nor is it about sales. Rather, it is about how sales and marketing work together to maximize growth, profitability, and customer value. Sales execution, within the framework of Structured Selling, is the pinnacle of that effort.

Facts to Remember

- One of the principles of a relationship marketing environment is that marketing acts in support of sales, *not* in spite of sales.
- Structured Selling is a system for boosting sales results by implementing the four major components of relationship selling—account planning, marketing programs, sales calls, and ongoing interactions.
- Marketing plays start with specific objectives. These objectives may be customer-focused, aimed at particular spaces on the conquest-grow-own Customer Relationship Continuum, or they may be product-focused, designed to affect the sales of specific products.

- Whatever your specific sales methodology, its purpose is going to be to identify, attract, develop, and own high lifetime value customers. The Structured Selling technique increases your chances at each stage of this process, none more so than when you are actually in front of a customer making your sales presentation.
- The Direct Impact Growth System is about creating rapid, profitable, sustainable growth—not getting one-time sales with limited profitability and doubtful prospects for long-term relationship-building. That's why ongoing interaction with targeted accounts is a pillar of Structured Selling.
- Sales execution is a multifaceted responsibility entailing conducting the required calls and presentations, meeting deadlines, communicating expectations, and managing the sales team and adjusting on-the-fly to react to response levels and other issues that crop up.
- Measurement and tracking in a Direct Impact Growth system is primarily intended to feedback information into the system so that objectives and techniques can be adjusted to reflect real-world performance of marketing and sales initiatives. As such, measurement and tracking is central to sales execution.

Part III

EVALUATION AND MODIFICATION

STEP

9

Metrics

Dell Computer's success today is, to a considerable degree, due to metrics. That may sound like a strong statement. How can measurement influence performance so much? But the statement is true in more ways than one. Take, for instance, financial performance metrics. In 1994, Dell posted a $39 million loss and was under attack by securities analysts for growing too fast and burning too much cash. Things got worse as Dell's inventory swelled and it had to write down millions of dollars of obsolescent inventory.

Then CFO Tom Meredith began focusing employees on the importance of measuring and improving Dell's cash conversion cycle, which is the length of time required to convert raw materials into sales and cash. Within a few years, the cycle shrank from 40 days—a mark many companies consider acceptable—to a negative 8 days. Negative eight days meant that customers were paying for assembled products prior to Dell's actual purchase of the components required to build them. As analysts began paying attention to Dell's striking cash conversion cycle numbers, and the rocketlike growth its freedom from cash constraints would allow, the stock resumed the ascent that made Dell famous during the 1990s.

In a similar manner, marketing metrics have been crucial to Dell's success. During Janet's years at Dell, spanning that same period, she created its first marketing program measurement systems. The measurement initiatives she introduced were based on the same basic idea: You can't change behavior unless you measure behavior. And you can't just measure customer and prospect response. You have to measure every aspect of your campaign and your prospects' behavior.

Metrics allowed her and other Dell marketers to try a wide range of marketing initiatives and finely tune those approaches that worked well. As a testament to measurement's value, Dell has continued and expanded the marketing metrics initiatives Janet began. Today Dell boasts refined marketing performance metrics that provide instant alerts to potential market problems with any product line in its global markets.

Dell's metrics keeps the company in contact with its ongoing performance. Similarly, all marketers must stay in touch with the performance of their programs by measuring the good, the bad, and the ugly of every campaign and every promotion made to the market. Measurement is the only way to know what's working and what's not and how to optimize or correct your campaign.

Measuring the results of your marketing in a detailed way is a hallmark of direct marketing. The ability to measure the inputs and outcomes of your marketing is absolutely essential to making intelligent decisions about which efforts to continue and expand, which ones to modify or abandon. The Direct Impact Growth System provides you with the information you need to control and direct your marketing efforts by measuring them comprehensively.

A critical feature of the Direct Impact Growth System (DIGS) and, indeed, all direct marketing is that it is intended to generate a response. Unlike advertising, which may be aimed at simply increasing awareness of a product or service among a general audience, direct marketing motivates its targets to take a specific action. This is an important distinction because, while a mass marketer may have difficulty identifying measurable results from a campaign, direct marketers should be able to measure every outcome of their campaigns. Good direct marketers measure every telephone call from prospects, every Web site visit, every request for samples, every order from a regular customer, or any number of other desirable outcomes.

Measurement is also integral to Organizational Magnification. This, as explained in detail in Step 6, is what happens when you get the whole company to understand, focus, and execute against a clear set of corporate objectives, saying the same thing, and behaving the same way.

Without adequate, accurate information about how your marketing efforts are faring, you can't achieve the powerful benefits of Organization Magnification because your employees won't fully understand how their actions affect your business. When your troops can point to concrete success as a result of their efforts, they are motivated to continue to execute against the goals you have established.

This is especially true of your sales team. Their compensation is often directly tied to the results of a sales and marketing campaign; constant factual feedback relating the campaign's results is an essential component of your campaign's success or failure.

If you have had any in-depth experience in direct marketing, you've probably done a variety of breakeven analyses, looked at the gross response and net response for a campaign, figured cost-per-inquiry and cost per order, and done a hundred other conventional direct marketing calculations. These are important metrics, but they don't provide you with the insight you need to manage your business in today's more volatile markets. DIGS goes beyond conventional marketing metrics to measure six major areas of marketing effectiveness:

1. Operational systems,
2. Market management systems,

3. Business health indicators,
4. Opportunity indicators,
5. Promotion histories, and
6. Responses.

Today, businesses that succeed are businesses that adapt. Measuring every aspect of your sales and marketing efforts allows you to spot changes in customers', prospects', and market's behavior. Seeing these changes lets you exploit the change and create a sustainable market advantage. By identifying and measuring these discrepancies, you can exploit the change and leverage a sustainable advantage in the marketplace.

Operational Systems

We'd like to nominate operational systems as the fourth major element of any direct marketing campaign alongside offer, creative, and list. Operational systems refer to the people, the technology, the processes, and the other resources you have dedicated to handle the anticipated response to any of your direct marketing campaigns. You can't take these operational systems for granted. At Micron, marketers secured toll-free numbers to use in a campaign without checking on the status of the numbers. Only later was it found that those numbers had been recycled and were, in fact, still in use by another advertising campaign. As a result, the outcomes of their direct marketing campaign were skewed.

The first step in metrics is to have all your operational systems in place and fully tested and to have all personnel who will touch customers fully trained and motivated. Verifying that your operational systems are in place, prepared, and can handle your expected response prior to the launching of your campaign is vital to the success of your campaign. Measuring the efficiency and effectiveness of your operational systems during a campaign is the prudent way to improve on future executions.

It's important to stress the steps that must be taken *in advance* of the campaign. Direct marketing is intended to generate a behavior, such as a customer inquiry. This requirement for generating actions means direct marketers must be ready to handle these actions with operational systems of several varieties.

Only measurement of the efficiency and effectiveness of operations in advance of a marketing effort will allow you to know with confidence that your operational systems are up to the task of handling inquiries, orders, and other interactions with customers and prospects sufficient to allow the campaign to perform against projected objectives.

Inbound telephone calls from customers and prospects are one manifestation of a direct marketing campaign. If your marketing is intended to spur telephone inquiries, you must have call centers equipped and staffed with enough trained operators to handle the expected influx. Recording and monitoring information such as the number of calls received, the time required to answer a call, time spent on a call, and number of operators required at peak calling times will help you ensure a positive experience for customers and prospects who dial your number.

Many marketing efforts today will have large numbers of information-seeking e-mail messages to answer in a reliable and timely fashion. You will want to measure and evaluate the number and rate of e-mail responses received for a campaign to determine whether your e-mail response system will perform against objectives.

People do not want to wait a long time for a Web page to load because its server is overloaded. If they get a "404" error indicating the page could not be accessed at all, they are likely to never attempt to return to that Web address. In short, Web sites must be capable of handling your projected volumes of visitors. Server software records, analyzes, and delivers reports on Web site traffic and performance in near real-time. Track these reports to see if your Web site hits are following predicted trends and whether your servers can cope with the traffic.

The goal of many direct marketing efforts is to get orders. With that in mind, even the most rudimentary measurement and tracking plan must focus on knowing, as soon and as fully as possible, how many orders are being placed. If you are pulling traffic to an online retail site, you will track how many shopping baskets are being created.

For all these operational systems tracking efforts, keep an eye on peaks. Customer and prospect interaction rarely follows a smooth, level track. Your peaks may occur during the workday, at night and on weekends, or almost any other time. The important thing is to know when the heaviest volume is occurring. The last thing you want is for customers to be unable to conveniently reach you, just when they most want to, because you haven't paid attention to the operational systems supporting your marketing efforts.

Market Management Systems

In the Overview, we introduced the idea of a Market Management System as an integrated, closed-loop sales and marketing contact system delivering relevant messages to selected targets resulting in maximum sales and deepened relationships at minimum costs.

At its simplest, the indispensable skill of managing a market is all about making sure that the influx of desirable new customers matches or exceeds the outflow of lost customers. And you can't know whether you are managing your market adequately unless you observe the trend of activities in market management systems. Market Management System metrics should track new customer acquisitions, customer defections, and customer spending levels.

Attracting desirable new customers should be a primary focus of your direct marketing efforts. While many marketing programs are intended to obtain growth by spurring additional activities from current customers, direct marketing's chief goal is to generate new customers. Given the inevitable attrition rates due to customers leaving the market, defecting to rivals, and otherwise becoming unavailable, all businesses must sooner or later attract new customers. Your measurement systems should flag and track new prospects as they become customers. You must be able to tell how many new faces are showing up in your sales figures, as well as when, where, and what the trends are.

Spending level is another center of interest. Not all customers are created equal and, as a general rule, those who spend more become your desirable segments. To determine whether the customers you are attracting are going to drive dollar sales volume up or just create unproductive churning, you must have a detailed understanding of their spending levels. Specifically, you should be able to segment customers into multiple groups including:

1. Those spending more than before,
2. Those spending more than average,
3. Those spending less, and
4. Those spending the same amount.

Understanding these dynamics allows you to set specific goals for each of these groups, execute specific campaigns, and test specific offers to see if you can create positive movement within each of these behavioral segments.

Nobody likes to think about losing customers, but every business loses customers nonetheless. This is one of those pieces of data that, even if uncomfortable to contemplate, is far better to know than to not know. When existing customers stop ordering, you have to be able to spot it, identify the specific customers, know when they stopped ordering, and how much lost sales volume they represent. This attrition rate will also include customers who are no longer being sold to because they have failed to pay for past orders.

Business Health Indicators

One of the ailments afflicting Mercedes-Benz was a long, steady, undetected decline in the loyalty rates of their customers. The fact that this decline was not identified nor appreciated by senior executives may be more important than the fact the slowdown occurred. A drop in activity by current customers can be dealt with by finding new customers or by refining products to encourage current customers to become more active. Because adequate measurement systems were not in place, this persistent decline resulted in an unpleasant and almost irreversible slide.

Your Direct Impact Growth System should provide for accurately measuring important indicators for the health of your business relating to customer activity and sales success. Business health indicators include information about the number of your customers who are active, the activities of flagship customers, ratios of new customers to lost customers, close rates, and average order value in addition to sales figures.

One primary axiom is that a body in motion tends to remain in motion. Put another way, the trend is your friend. Your measurement and tracking system for business health indicators should yield accurate, up-to-date information about the trends in your customer base. To begin with, you need to know the percentage of your customers who are active. Depending on what you are selling, this may mean they have placed an order in the past week, month, quarter, year, or even longer period. Purchasers of capital items such as heavy equipment do not place orders as often as, say, customers buying groceries. The vital ingredient is to know whether or not your customers are active and if their activity is changing. A sharp or sustained falloff in the activity levels of customers can be a sign that something is seriously amiss.

Now let's return to the theme of Value Segmentation. Your business health indicators need to be able to discriminate among customer activities depending on whether the customers are of high, medium, or low value. Just as the Dow Jones Industrial Average indicates the overall performance of the stock market, you'll want to identify some flagship accounts in each of your Value Segmentation Matrix quadrants. Usually you will be most interested in high-value customers, although the movement of low-value customers upward to the medium-value range (and vice versa) will also be of concern.

Creating relevant ratios that help translate the analysis into something your entire organization understands and can relate to is important as well. For instance, the ratio of new customers to lost customers will give you insight into trends affecting the long-term growth or diminution of your customer base. Similarly, looking at the ratio of customers who are more active in relation to those who are less active will tell you whether you are communicating appropriately to a desirable pool of prospects, or whether you need to tailor your marketing to change that ratio.

Before customer relationship management took on such a high profile, the first and sometimes only quantity marketers and businesses were interested in was actual sales. We know a variety of things affect customer relationships, so we pay more attention to them. Still, we need to know what actual sales are. Your monitoring system should provide actual sales data in conjunction with other business health numbers to help you perceive them in context.

Average order value is a business health metric that has important implications about the financial feasibility of your marketing efforts. Average order values must remain at or above a certain level to justify the investments you are making in acquiring each account. If average order values slip below economically viable levels, or are trending that way, you are going to have to change your marketing model or take other steps to avoid the looming trouble.

The pace of orders provides crucial feedback for making sure that all aspects of your marketing campaign are appropriately set up. If orders are rapidly ramping up, you must recognize it before they reach a level that will stress your order-taking capabilities. If they are falling off or tending to fluctuate in a predictable fashion—peaking on weekends, say, and declining during the week—you must use this information to optimize staffing and response components to their most profitable levels.

The rate at which sales are being closed by marketing efforts controls the overall financial viability of your marketing efforts. This all ties back to your corporate objectives. If close rates are low, you may not be able to spend enough money on direct marketing to reach enough prospects to generate the desired financial results. Knowing this, you can take action to improve close rates by improving marketing support tools provided to salespeople, or by modifying your expected results to fit projected outcomes. You can, for instance, refine your target audience or reset your expected results to reflect this deficiency in your campaign.

Opportunity Indicators

DIGS allows you to develop knowledge about and relationships with individual customers. To know whether you are achieving this important goal, track opportunity indicators. Opportunity indicators include the number of customers buying more than one product category, the number of customers buying the optimum number of products and the number of customers buying above or below industry averages.

How many of your customers are buying more than one product category from you? The range of likely answers is going to depend on your industry and on how many product categories you offer. You must know this before you can tune your marketing machine to produce acceptable returns.

Track as well the percentage of your customers who are buying the number of products—call it N—that you have determined represents the optimum for your business. You want the portion of your customers reaching the N level to go up, and you want to know it's happening (or isn't). You can consult a variety of industry resources to establish industry averages. Once you establish industry averages, you can see if your customers and prospects are performing above or below these averages.

Promotion Histories

The great power of direct marketing lies in your ability to precisely measure results and connect them to specific promotions. This gives you the opportunity to fine-tune future efforts to produce better and better results. You can't do this without a record of the promotion history, including the number of times a product or service has been promoted, the cost of promotions, specific products and services promoted, timing of promotions, methods of promotion, and other details.

You should know the number of times you have promoted a product or service. Most items require more than one promotion to secure a sale. Counting the number of direct mail letters, e-mail messages, outbound telemarketing calls, space ads, and other promotions you conduct is necessary if you are to adhere to the pro forma you have built. It's also necessary to identify what works and what it costs to generate an order.

The cost of promotions is not necessarily expressed in terms of the overall cost of the promotion. Instead, it's useful to look at what each promotion costs in terms of the number of orders each effort generated. Track and measure this number and you'll be able to intelligently compare the cost-effectiveness of all of your different methods of promotion.

In addition to studying your promotional methods, you need to examine the specific products and services you are promoting. Selecting the right target, having accurate information, and crafting an appealing offer are important, but the suitability of the products and services you are selling decides how well your company performs over the long term. It's also important to match promotions with the right products and services. Even an outstanding product may fail if it is not properly promoted. So track promotions as they relate to your products and services as well.

Timing in promotion isn't everything, but it is significant. In addition to obvious factors such as seasonality, you need to consider the specific time of day your promotions will run and the media that you are using. If you are promoting via radio, drive time is likely your most profitable time to advertise. Adding time of promotion to your metrics gives you the information you need to assess and adjust your media purchases and promotional spends.

The first cut at surveying your method of promotion is to look at whether you are using direct mail, space advertising, broadcast promotion, telemarketing, or e-mail based promotions. These methods of promotion vary in important ways, not the least of which is cost. The cost of contacting someone via a telemarketing call is many times the cost of contacting them via direct mail, which is many times the cost of contacting them via e-mail. Least costly of all is space advertising. Space advertising also, in raw numbers, generally is the least effective means of promotion, meaning you will get fewer prospects and customers per person reached. Space advertising's low costs can make it a viable means of promoting many mail-order and other products and services. By taking note of your means of promotion, you can find out whether less costly promotions are effective and if they have a significant effect on your promotion's bottom line. Also, in addition to looking at what method you are using to promote, look at details of each promotional vehicle. For instance, examine the results of using simple direct mail postcards as well as more complex direct mail packages consisting of a multipage letter, brochure, order form, and other components. What you find may surprise you, and most definitely should affect your future campaigns.

Responses

Direct marketing isn't working unless it seeks and generates responses from customers and prospects. Observing the nature of the responses you receive from customers is vital to making sure you are getting at least the required number necessary to justify the effort. Response measures to track include response method, timing of responses, products selected by segment, method of payment, and the number of inquiries versus purchases.

Start by looking at the method of the response. This is something you can and probably will attempt to control by encouraging targets to dial a toll-free number. However, not all customers and prospects will want to contact you this way. Offering appropriate avenues of response is critical. If you are reaching targets via a Web site, e-mail is the natural response method. If you are buying space in the Sunday newspaper, a call center staffed 24 hours a day, seven days a week (24/7) may be necessary for you to adequately service your respondents.

The options your target audience chooses will tell you much about your marketing efforts and customers. If your Web site is intended to drive foot traffic to your local retail establishment, but you find you are generating unexpected numbers of e-mails and telephone calls, you may have to adjust your approach and message.

The time of responses can give you valuable insight into how to coordinate the various aspects of a marketing campaign. For instance, if inbound telephone calls responding to a direct mailing begin to come in no sooner than two days after the second mailing, you would probably be wise in not contacting recipients of these mailings prior to two days after the mailing. In this manner, tracking time of response can make a big difference in the effectiveness of your salesforce.

Good direct marketing provides prospects more than one product to choose from. With that in mind, noting the products selected by specific segments in response to specific promotions is invaluable for evaluating product appeal and promotion effectiveness.

You can profitably track the method of payment selected by customers as well. This information helps you decide which payment methods to offer—credit card, check—and can also predict the eventual profitability of a campaign. For instance, payment is more certain when purchasers pay by credit card, because the purchase price is applied immediately to the card's balance, thereby eliminating the risk of bad checks. A campaign that is attracting an unusually high number of credit card payments might be more profitable than a similar campaign where checks are more popular.

Marketing efforts can place products and services in front of appropriate prospects and provide potential customers with information and assistance in reaching a buying decision. But if there is a problem with the product, price, or other part of the offer, marketing can't make someone buy. That's why it's important to know the percentage of people contacted who are inquiring about your product, but wind up not buying. Understanding this information is vital for product design and manufacturing executions so they can determine if changes or improvements need to be made to make the product successful.

Bottom-Line Metrics

Ultimately, you decide what to measure. It may be appropriate for you to follow all the metrics discussed, a much smaller subset, or even a greater number. Corporate and departmental objectives should drive your selection of marketing metrics.

If your paramount corporate goal is to find new customers, for instance, then clearly you have to measure and manage the new customer number. What helps you to improve your business is a matter for you to decide in the context of corporate objectives and within the limitations of what is measurable—you may not, for instance, be able to determine exactly why a given promotion isn't effective. Knowing that it isn't, however, may be just as useful.

Don't limit yourself to measuring just the things we've mentioned. Instead, explore all possibilities relating to any issue that is important to your organization. For instance, rates of product returns may have a profound effect on the bottom line of your organization. This information can provide valuable insight into the market's acceptance of your products and services. You may want to look at other transactional components—bad debt, support calls received, customer satisfaction, and so on.

The essence of marketing metrics is to be aware of the drivers of your business. Once identified, find a way to measure them. Only by measuring performance can you change performance.

Facts to Remember

- Measuring the results of your marketing in a detailed way is a hallmark of direct marketing. The ability to measure the inputs and outcomes of your marketing is absolutely essential to making intelligent decisions about which efforts to continue and expand, which ones to modify or abandon. The Direct Impact Growth System provides you with the information you need to control and direct your marketing efforts by measuring them comprehensively.
- Without adequate, accurate information about how your marketing efforts are faring, you can't achieve the powerful benefits of Organization Magnification because your employees won't fully understand how their actions affect your business. When your employees can point to concrete success as a result of their efforts, they are motivated to continue to execute against the goals you have established.

(Continued)

- DIGS goes beyond conventional marketing metrics to measure six major areas of marketing effectiveness: operational systems, market management systems, business health indicators, opportunity indicators, promotion histories, and responses.
- Only measurement of the efficiency and effectiveness of operations in advance of a marketing effort will allow you to know with confidence that your operational systems are up to the task of handling inquiries, orders, and other interactions with customers and prospects sufficient to allow the campaign to perform against projected objectives.
- At its simplest, the indispensable skill of managing a market is all about making sure that the influx of desirable new customers matches or exceeds the outflow of lost customers. You can't know whether you are managing your market adequately unless you observe the trend of activities in market management systems. Market Management System metrics should track new customer acquisitions, customer defections, and customer spending levels.
- DIGS should provide for accurately measuring important indicators for the health of your business relating to customer activity and sales success. Business health indicators include information about the number of your customers who are active, the activities of flagship customers, ratios of new customers to lost customers, close rates, and average order value in addition to sales figures.
- DIGS allows you to develop knowledge about and relationships with individual customers. To know whether you are achieving this important goal, track opportunity indicators. Opportunity indicators include the number

of customers buying more than one product category, the number of customers buying the optimum number of products, and the number of customers buying above or below industry averages.

- The great power of direct marketing lies in your ability to precisely measure results and connect them to specific promotions. This gives you the opportunity to fine-tune future efforts to produce better and better results. You can't do this without a record of the promotion history, including the number of times a product or service has been promoted, the cost of promotions, specific products and services promoted, timing of promotions, methods of promotion, and other promotion details.
- Direct marketing isn't direct marketing unless it seeks and generates responses from customers and prospects. Observing the nature of the responses you receive from customers is vital to making sure you are getting at least the required number necessary to justify the effort. Response measures to track include response method, timing of responses, products selected by segment, method of payment, and the number of inquiries versus purchases.
- Ultimately, you decide what to measure. It may be appropriate for you to follow all the metrics cited, a much smaller subset, or even a greater number. Corporate and departmental objectives should drive your selection of marketing metrics.

STEP

10

Closing the Loop

Closing the loop seems to be something almost everybody wants to do in some form or another. Information technologists speak of closing the loop with software that monitors system failures and alerts technicians to problems requiring repair. Environmentalists want to create closed-loop economies by reducing, reusing, and recycling resources. Meat producers even speak of a livestock identification system that tracks food products from farm to consumer as closing the loop. Clearly, closing the loop means different things to different people.

The first terms in the definition of the Direct Impact Growth System (DIGS) presented in the Overview described it as a closed-loop system of marketing. What do we mean by closing the loop in marketing?

Closing the loop in the Direct Impact Growth System is a matter of using the insights gained by your implementation as intelligent feedback to allow you to modify your Market Management System and refine your corporate objectives.

Although we've waited until the final chapter to discuss closing the loop, this is emphatically one of those cases where last is not least. Closing the loop by feeding back knowledge and understanding gained from using the DIGS is an integral part of its implementation. According to philosopher George Santayana, "Those who do not remember the past are condemned to repeat it." We would modify that to: Those who do not remember the past, and try to learn from it, are doomed to repeat it without improving results. In a highly competitive, globally open, continuously improving environment, failure to improve results is a recipe for failing utterly. The practice of closing the marketing loop is designed to, more than just avoid failure, create the conditions for outsized sales growth and success.

Obtaining Results

The financial results you get from the finance department may not be exactly what you need to evaluate and modify your marketing. A simple quarterly profit-and-loss statement, even if broken out by line of business, isn't detailed enough to help you here. In Step 5 we went through the process of preparing a pro forma to help us project how a marketing effort will perform. You need to know the kind of information that went into your pro forma before you can effectively adjust your marketing to achieve the kind of financial results you require.

The building blocks of pro formas are assumptions. What you are after now are the actual results, which will help you develop more and, hopefully, better forward-looking assumptions.

Start by examining how well your estimate of Allowable Budget measured up to reality. You'll want to see that Unit Revenue came in close to projections. If it's lower than you expected, it may be due to excessively discounted sales of products. If it's higher then you may be selling richer configurations of products than you thought you would.

Closing the loop means thinking of all components of your pro forma as intertwined, each affecting others, which in turn affect still others. It's clear that changes in Unit Revenue will affect all actual results that follow. Any significant changes from projections will give you a bigger or smaller budget for marketing. If revenues go up to $16,000 per unit, as long as the percent of revenue allowed for marketing remains the same, a higher or lower revenue per unit will change the marketing budget per unit. You may need to change the revenue percentage allocated to marketing if the budget is inadequate. The pro forma in Figure 10.1 shows how a pro forma may change if key elements come in differently than you projected. This version of a pro forma includes a column for actual outcomes, along with a column providing possible explanations of the altered outcomes.

When the actual revenues per unit rise, the allowable promotion budget per unit rises to $800, based on higher unit revenues and a constant 5 percent allocation for marketing. The formula is

$$\text{Budget per unit} = \text{Percent of revenue allowed} \times \text{Unit revenue}$$

Figure 10.1 Marketing Pro Forma Reconciliation

Allowable Budget	Assumptions	Actuals	Possible Explanation
• Unit revenue	$ 15,000	$ 16,000	• Fewer volume discounts to large buyers
• Percent of revenue allowed	5%	5%	
• Budget per unit	$ 750	$ 800	
Budget Allocation			
• Targets	250,000	250,000	
• Response rates	3%	3%	
• Close rates	35%	35%	
• Units sold	2,625	2,625	
• Promotion budget	$1,968,750	$2,100,000	• Higher budget per unit
• Average times promoted	3	3	
• Allowable promo/person	$2.63	$2.80	

If unit revenue had risen to $17,000, then $17,000 times 5 percent equals a budget per unit figure of $850. If unit revenues decrease, lower promotion budgets result. Unit revenues of $14,000 would result in a promotion budget per unit of $700. Let's look at what happens in the rest of the pro forma as unit revenue rises to $16,000.

Higher unit revenue affects the entire pro forma, enabling you to upgrade the quality of your mail piece, test expanded markets, increase the number of times you promote, and so on. These enhancements can drive the success of the whole campaign to a much higher level. Similarly, lower unit revenues can reduce the amount of resources you can expend on marketing, perhaps making it difficult to achieve forecast results. Figure 10.2 shows how the pro forma promotion budget would be affected by a drop in unit revenue to $14,000.

This step concerns itself not just with the way outcomes can vary, but with what you can learn from changes in outcomes. It's not enough to know what happened. The question you should be asking yourself once you have an actual unit revenue figure in hand is: Why is this number different from the assumptions in the original

Figure 10.2 Marketing Pro Forma Reconciliation

Allowable Budget	Assumptions	Actuals	Possible Explanation
• Unit revenue	$ 15,000	$ 14,000	• Competitor's new product announcement occurred during the rollout of our campaign
• Percent of revenue allowed	5%	5%	
• Budget per unit	$ 750	$ 700	
Budget Allocation			
• Targets	250,000	250,000	
• Response rates	3%	3%	
• Close rates	35%	35%	
• Units sold	2,625	2,625	
• Promotion budget	$1,968,750	$1,837,500	• Reduced due to volume discount with new printer
• Average times promoted	3	3	
• Allowable promo/person	$2.63	$2.45	

pro forma? In this case, a possible explanation is that large buyers were granted fewer discounts from the regular price for the units. Note that the explanation itself may raise additional questions: Why were big customers granted fewer discounts? Was overall demand higher than expected? Did expected competitive presence fail to materialize? Asking and answering these questions will enable you to tailor your next marketing effort to produce more predictable and profitable results.

Differences in assumed and actual unit revenues are important, but any of the assumptions you make in your pro forma are subject to change when your plans collide with the real world. The pro forma in Figure 10.3 illustrates the effect of several possible revisions to results.

Look first at the actual number of targets that you reached. In this case, the number of targets you were after shrank significantly. The possible explanation is that the process of updating, eliminating duplicates, and otherwise cleaning the data resulted in 10 percent fewer good names to contact.

Figure 10.3 Marketing Pro Forma Reconciliation

Allowable Budget	Assumptions	Actuals	Possible Explanation
• Unit revenue	$ 15,000	$ 16,000	• Fewer volume discounts to large buyers
• Percent of revenue allowed	5%	5%	
• Budget per unit	$ 750	$ 800	
Budget Allocation			
• Targets	250,000	225,000	• List shrinkage after data cleansing
• Response rates	3%	3.50%	• Higher response due to cleaner list
• Close rates	35%	40%	• Closing tools more effective
• Units sold	2,625	3,150	• Better response and close rates
• Promotion budget	$1,968,750	$2,520,000	• Higher budget per unit and greater number of units sold
• Average times promoted	3	3.1	• Second phone call required for 25,000 targets
• Allowable promo/person	$2.63	$3.61	• Smaller number of targets in campaign

Response rate clearly is another key number. If it's higher than projected, you can usually expect a more successful marketing effort. Figure 10.3 illustrates the effect of an increase in response rate from 3 percent to 3.5 percent. This change is possibly explained by the data cleansing that reduced the number of targets.

Another change from assumption to actual results in this pro forma is the close rate. The marketer explained the increase in the rate from an assumed 35 percent to an actual 40 percent as a result of having more effective closing tools. You should drill down for more detail. Which tools seemed to generate the improved rate? Was there something about these that could be expanded and applied elsewhere in the closing tool kit or in the overall campaign?

When close rate goes up, the units sold figure also rises sharply, even given the lower number of targets. The 22 percent increase in units sold over assumptions in this pro forma is an increase that could affect far more than the strictly marketing concerns reflected in the pro forma. Units sold must be taken into consideration as far upstream as ordering raw materials, supplies, and parts for manufacturing, and as far downstream as staffing customer service and warranty centers. To give one example, if you are selling more units than you can comfortably supply, you may want to adjust selling prices, size of target market, or other factors to restrain demand.

The promotion budget must be considered if the marketing effort is to be financially successful, but that doesn't mean you have to slavishly stick to what you estimated in your pro forma. If you are generating extra promotion dollars through higher-than-expected sales, not using them may be a waste of opportunity. If, on the other hand, your promotion budget isn't measuring up due to slower unit sales or revenues, then you'll have to rein in your plans or risk falling short on the bottom line.

Response and close rates are likely to be strongly affected by the average times promoted figure. This number itself should be easily controllable by you, but you may find it necessary to turn up the heat, contacting prospects additional times by whatever means is affordable and appropriate, if other numbers such as unit sales aren't coming in on budget. Allowable promotion per person will then be modified appropriately.

Other Financial Considerations

Your Contact Plan is subject to on-the-fly revision as results are registered. Examine the results for the segments you have identified and the strategies you have selected for them and implement specific changes in your next campaign (Figure 10.4).

As in the case of the pro forma, the entire Contact Plan is sensitive to changes in any of the figures representing the assumptions you used to build it. Let us say that you find that the assault segment more accurately contains 45,000 targets, while the develop group consists of 60,000 prospects and customers. This small change makes a difference of 44 in the number of units sold (Figure 10.5). At the unit revenue of $15,000 used in the pro forma, this brings another $660,000 to the top line. Any changes in the budget per name, response per segment, or close per segment will have significant multiplier effects.

You can apply what you have learned and adjust your Contact Plan for future campaigns by changing the number of times you plan to contact members of segments or by taking steps to improve response and close rates. Let us assume that you try to boost your

Figure 10.4 Contact Plan

Segment	$$$	$$	$	Totals
Contacts	MMECP	MECP	MM	$3.18
Circulation	40,000	65,000	145,000	250,000
Budget/Name	$13.13	$10.50	$5.25	$2.63
Budget/Segment	$525,200	$682,500	$761,250	$1,968,950
Response/Segment	6.00%	2.50%	2.00%	2.77%
Close/Segment	35%	35%	35%	35%
Units	840	796	1,015	2,651

Figure 10.5 Contact Plan

Segment	$$$	$$	$	Totals
Contacts	MMMCM	MMCM	MM	
Circulation	45,000	60,000	145,000	250,000
Budget/Name	$13.13	$10.50	$5.25	
Budget/Segment	$590,850	$630,000	$761,250	$1,982,100
Response/Segment	6.00%	3.50%	2.00%	
Close/Segment	35%	35%	35%	35%
Units	945	735	1,015	2,695

response rate for Segment 3 by adding an additional e-mail contact to the two direct-mail contacts budgeted for in your original Contact Plan (Figure 10.6). This increases the budget per name for Segment 3 to $5.57 and raises the response rate for that segment by one quarter of a percentage point. Result: Total unit sales increase to 2,822, generating another $2.5 million in revenues to help make up for the bigger marketing expense.

Closed loop means revisiting in a candid and open manner with all departments involved in a campaign. This may be painful, but it's necessary to be successful. Do not stop your evaluation and adjustments based on financial results of your own analysis. As you did in originally gathering input on the marketing effort, survey the audiences you are dealing with to find out what their needs are and how those needs may have changed.

Figure 10.6 Contact Plan

Segment	$$$	$$	$	Totals
Contacts	MMMCM	MMCM	MEM	
Circulation	45,000	60,000	145,000	250,000
Budget/Name	$13.13	$10.50	$5.75	
Budget/Segment	$590,850	$630,000	$797,500	$2,018,350
Response/Segment	6.00%	3.50%	2.25%	
Close/Segment	35%	35%	35%	35%
Units	945	735	1,142	2,822

Share results with appropriate people in your organization to obtain input on ways to improve subpar outcomes and take advantage of unforeseen opportunities. Confer with salespeople to try to determine pricing elasticity—can you get by with a higher price? If the sales price needs to be lower—by how much? What effect will it have on the pro forma? You can do focus groups and surveys of customer and prospect groups to help find ways to increase response rates, get ideas for improved closing tools for salespeople, and other initiatives that can boost financial results.

Tweaking a marketing campaign is more than changing cells in a spreadsheet for a pro forma. You must consider the timing of adjustments you have determined you want to make. Should changes be made midcampaign? Or should you wait for a fresh campaign? Take care in how and when you make adjustments. Sometimes it's better to take the lessons you have learned and apply them next time rather than risk confusing customers and prospects, alienating salespeople, or hampering organizational magnification by changing your strategy midstream.

There is always a risk of oversteering—especially when a campaign is skidding badly. Markets are complex systems. When you add such ineffable factors such as brand image, price sensitivity, and information overload to the powerful leveraging effects of taking actions such as increasing numbers of promotional contacts, you can have a significant, even disastrous, effect on the outcome of your efforts. Proceed with caution, creating what-if models of every change you make and staying in touch with salespeople, finance, production, and other concerned parties to try to assess accurately the effects of any changes you are about to make.

Modifying Your Database

Examine the information in your database. Would expanding or freshening it possibly help increase response rates or provide more accurate value segmentation? In Step 2 we described the three fatal mistakes most marketers make in designing and building marketing information databases. When it comes to closing the loop, we would add a fourth. They:

1. Don't know what they're going to do with it.
2. Don't have a plan for keeping it fresh.
3. Don't build it with access in mind.
4. Build in components that can't be measured.

Ideally, you have avoided the worst of these pitfalls. But you probably still have some areas where you could do better. With that in mind, ask yourself: Did we maximize the use of our market management system? If not, perhaps you misunderstood the role a database can play in your marketing effort. It's likely that the potential was not realized because the information in the marketing database was not accurate, complete, or up to date.

Approach examination of your database with a positive attitude—it is common to find that you can dispense with some information because it is no longer being used nor is it likely to ever be used. Reducing the depth of your database may allow you to add new categories of information, purchase better supplemental data from external sources, or to do more frequent updates. Reducing the number of fields in a database may reduce complexity. That can cut training and maintenance costs, freeing up additional dollars for productive uses.

By now, you should have a good idea of whether the information in your database is being adequately updated. This is likely to be a critical issue. If you are experiencing unacceptably high numbers of "return to sender," then the culprit is likely to be a failing in your plan for keeping your data fresh. You can increase the frequency and scope of your updating activities, such as scheduling specific days for salespeople to call all contacts and update their data. You can build these efforts into regular marketing and business activities by having service personnel gather information about the number of installed units at a site each time they are called for help with a problem. This information must be added to the database in a timely fashion.

Now is the time to recheck whether the islands of data in your organization have been integrated. Have inconsistencies in the data been accurately reconciled? Information obtained must be accurately linked for your database to be truly useful. Crosscheck to find out whether the contacts, addresses, account codes, and other key information match up within your database. As with the other adjustments you are making, you may find that your early plans overestimated the difficulty of integrating and reconciling database contents. You may be leaving value on the table by overinvesting in these areas and diverting resources from other, needier requirements.

Reporting

Examine carefully how the reports you have designed are being used. Do users say the reports answer their questions and provide them with the information and means to make decisions? Audit your reports for their utility and value. Trim unnecessary ones, identify, design, and add new ones as necessary. Examine the access to your database. If people have access to the database but aren't using it, you need to understand why.

You may, in the process of making your adjustments, find that the real problem with your marketing database lies not in its design but in the execution of its creation and scope. In this case, look at the system you set up for maintaining command of the process. Did you pick the right person to be your data czar project leader? Did you sufficiently monitor and reinforce the executive charged with sponsoring this project? Perhaps you didn't communicate the process to the person whose responsibility it was. Perhaps you, or your data czar (who may well be you), failed to impart to everyone in your organization how they were involved in the database and marketing efforts. If any of these occurred, now is the time to replace the leadership (even if it's you), to set up better monitoring and reinforcement systems and to make sure that everyone sees how his or her participation will positively affect the outcome.

Record and report your execution on all the process steps. Reset your expectations and, as always, plan in advance to close the loop again. When the next time for a review and adjustment occurs, remember: No database will ever be 100 percent correct. But that doesn't mean you can't get closer to that goal all the time.

Now that you've been through a complete turn of the database design-implementation-modification cycle, you're ready to employ another exceptionally powerful tool: That is, to end with the start in mind. As you evaluate your database, begin thinking now about ways to improve its future evaluation, redesign, and modification. Ending with the start in mind will reinforce and leverage the closed-loop nature of DIGS, helping you obtain the maximum possible sales level for the opportunities you face.

Modifying Your Corporate Objectives

Corporate objectives were a constantly moving target at Dell Computer. In the early 1990s, when Dell was still small enough to double in size each year or so, objectives were set accordingly. As company sales grew to several and then many billions of dollars a year, these goals had to be tempered to reflect reality. It simply wasn't possible for a $10 billion in sales company to double in the course of 12 months. It was, however, possible for Dell to vault from $889 million in fiscal 1992 sales to over $2 billion in revenues for 1993, as well as maintaining growth rates in excess of 50 percent for much of the 1990s. In fact, the company's prospects were so volatile that setting realistic objectives sometimes seemed more like an exercise in optimism than in realism. Dell is the exception. Few companies will consistently outstretch even the rosiest forecasts, as Dell has done for much of its history to date. Even now as we write this, Dell has had to implement cost-cutting activities to respond to the industry's economic downturn. Similarly, you can and should adjust your corporate objectives based on the feedback you are receiving from the metrics you have built into your implementation of the Direct Impact Growth System.

The combination of bottom-up and top-down objective setting described in Step 1 may have seemed exotic and unlikely when you first read about it. But, as one of the engines powering Dell Computer's remarkable decade of growth, it certainly deserves consideration by all companies. The good news is that now, with an intelligent database in place and with focus on organizational magnification and other components of DIGS, you are positioned to apply the broad-based objective setting technique employed at Dell.

Having a major investor, board of directors, CEO, or CFO tell you what the corporate results have to be without reference to market realities would be unacceptable. Armed with your well-honed knowledge of your markets, value segments, and the results of your integrated approach to marketing, you can rapidly evaluate top-down objective fiats for their workability. Furthermore, if it becomes necessary to challenge objectives that are driven by Wall Street expectations or other external factors, you will have the hard data to buttress your position. You can keep discussions of corporate objectives in the real world without being seen as a naysayer or unwillingly shouldering an unworkable responsibility.

Similarly, you won't be held hostage to unrealistically pessimistic projections emanating from salespeople who might be motivated by trying to keep their quotas low. By demonstrating that a target market has huge potential and required sales rates are obtainable, you can maintain territory quotas high without making your salesforce feel it is being asked to do the impossible.

Corporate objectives that are both doable and worth doing are within your hand when you employ market management through the Direct Impact Growth System. Using what you have learned now to reset corporate objectives will result in new goals that are more closely aligned with what is possible and what it required than you have probably ever been able to do before.

Ending Is Beginning

We began this book by recounting the story of Joe's Garage as a reinforcement of the maxim: Leverage thy customers, leverage every single one. Odds are good that your company, large or small, is not much like Joe's Garage, and the environment has changed enormously as well. But the fact remains that DIGS offers businesses unmatched ability to deal efficiently with global markets, while retaining the ability to select just the right groups of customers to concentrate on.

The purpose of this book has been more than to impart a detailed series of steps you can take to achieve rocketlike growth rates. In addition to describing the Direct Impact Growth System, we want to strongly make the point that companies often fail because they are selling great products at good prices to the wrong set of customers. Now, hopefully, you not only know how to optimize the right set of customers, you also know that you must target the right set.

There are many consistent themes in *Planting Flowers, Pulling Weeds,* but one we'd like to hit on one more time is the idea that Prospect Relationship Management is the primary engine of business growth. Customer Relationship Management (CRM) is an essential concept and has deservedly been a focal point for companies everywhere. But all the CRM in the world doesn't make people into automatons. Customers retain their free will and they will exercise it by changing suppliers from time to time. They also have finite needs—when you've sold them everything they can use, they cease being good customers. Testimonial and referral sources, maybe, but purchasers, not. The key point is that you can only rely on your current customer set for so long. Prospect Relationship Management fills the gap and is one of the most important abilities contained in the DIGS skill set.

Integration, coordination, and evolution are words that appear throughout this book. Sales and marketing efforts are unfortunately often regarded as a series of exercises to be executed in isolation from one another. That is far from ideal. Sales should be receptive to marketing's input, and marketing should operate in support of sales, not in spite of sales.

Your relationship marketing efforts must be well thought out, coordinated, and evolutionary, building on one another in a logical fashion. That' s why a key focus of this book is executing them in context, in a systematic approach, through the Direct Impact Growth System.

Our first image, even before we introduced Joe, raised the question of how your marketing is perceived by your customers and prospects. Odds are good that it did not come across as warmly or as authentically as old Joe in his grease-stained overalls. We've waited until now to say—so what? Today is not yesterday. It's not likely or appropriate that your organization, no matter how large or small, high-tech or low-tech, could or should embody the marketing ideals of a mid-twentieth-century service station. But it did serve to introduce the concept of leveraging your customers. And we'll use it again to help you come to grips with another idea, this one involving the future.

Today is tomorrow's past. The kind of marketing we're talking about will someday be perceived and presented as old-fashioned and hearkening back to a simpler time, when businesses had better relationships with customers. But marketers will, in fact, be dealing with many of the same issues. How to build customer relationships? How to extract maximum value from your customers. How to find new customers? What new marketing tools are available to help with those jobs? Today, the best answer to all those questions is *Planting Flowers, Pulling Weeds,* with the Direct Impact Growth System.

Facts to Remember

- Closing the loop in the Direct Impact Growth System is a matter of using the insights gained by your implementation as intelligent feedback to allow you to modify your Market Management System and refine your corporate objectives.
- The building blocks of pro formas are assumptions. What you are after now are the actual results, which will help you develop more and, hopefully, better forward-looking assumptions.
- Closed loop means revisiting in a candid and open manner with all departments involved in a campaign. This may be painful, but it's necessary to be successful. Do not stop your evaluation and adjustments based on financial results with your own analysis. As you did in originally gathering input on the marketing effort, survey the audiences you are dealing with to find out what their needs are and how those needs may have changed.
- Record and report your execution on all the process steps. Reset your expectations and, as always, plan in advance to close the loop again. When the next time for a review and adjustment occurs, remember: No database will ever be 100 percent correct. But that doesn't mean you can't get closer to that goal all the time.
- Corporate objectives that are both doable and worth doing are within your hand when you employ market management through the Direct Impact Growth System. Using what you have learned now to reset corporate objectives will result in new goals that are more closely aligned with what is possible and what it required than you have probably ever been able to do before.

❀ Your relationship marketing efforts must be well thought out, coordinated, and evolutionary, building on one another in a logical fashion. That' s why a key focus of this book is executing them in context, in a systematic approach, through the Direct Impact Growth System.

APPENDIX

Resources

Books

Direct Marketing Market Place
National Register Publishing, $324.99

An annually updated industry directory providing contact information on approximately 16,000 individual contacts and more than 10,000 direct marketers, service firms and suppliers.

Direct Marketing Rules of Thumb: 1,000 Practical and Profitable Ideas to Help You Improve Response, Save Money, and Increase Efficiency in Your Direct Program
By Nat G. Bodian
McGraw-Hill, $59.95

Laymen and experienced pros alike will benefit from this concise reference that covers all the basics from card packs and mailing lists to list brokers and letter shop techniques.

Tested Advertising Methods
By John Caples and Fred Hahn
Prentice Hall Trade, $14.95

Legendary marketer John Caples' classic book on creating successful advertising is updated here by consultant Fred Hahn. Specifics and sound advice.

Successful Direct Mail
By Liz Ferdi
Barron's Educational Series, $6.95

In only 100 pages, this concise guide takes you through the elements of creating a direct mail program, from matching product to market, selecting and readying lists and testing, to handling customer responses, measuring results, and more.

Response! The Complete Guide to Profitable Direct Marketing
By Lois K. Geller
Simon & Schuster, $25.00

Starting with the elements of an effective offer, direct marketing expert Lois Geller leads readers through identifying customers, fulfillment, budgeting, planning, and global marketing using tested direct marketing techniques.

Direct Marketing Success
By Freeman F. Gosden Jr.
John Wiley & Sons, $24.95

A nuts-and-bolts guide explaining concepts and techniques that make direct marketing work. Covers list selection, integrating with salesforce efforts, creating winning packages, and more.

The Complete Database Marketer: Second Generation Strategies and Techniques for Tapping the Power of Your Customer Database
By Arthur M. Hughes
McGraw-Hill, $54.95

A veteran database marketer walks you through the essentials of building and maintaining an effective database for building and maintaining customer relationships.

Profitable Direct Marketing
By Jim Kobs
NTC Publishing, $49.95

Author Jim Kobs here does a good job of covering both basic and advanced strategies for direct marketing.

Direct Mail Copy That Sells!
By Herschell Gordon Lewis
Prentice Hall Press, $14.95

The title is self-explanatory but it bears adding that this one is truly a classic. You'll find a copy on countless marketer's desks and bookshelves.

The World's Greatest Direct Mail Sales Letters
By Herschell Gordon Lewis and Carol Nelson
NTC Publishing Group, $79.95

Practical tips on writing sales letters in many industries with background information and samples of nearly 100 of the best-selling direct mail letters of all time.

Beyond 2000: The Future of Direct Marketing
By Jerry Reitman
NTC Publishing Group, $27.95

Though published in 1996 before the impact of the Internet was obvious, this book's vision of the future of direct marketing by 28 leading experts provides an interesting set of views on where technology will take marketers.

The New Direct Marketing: How to Implement a Profit-Driven Database Marketing Strategy, Third Edition
By David Shepard Associates
McGraw-Hill, $111.25

A complete overview of all areas of direct marketing with emphasis on the numbers. Covers fundamentals of targeting, modeling, and segmentation; technology, theory and economics of database marketing, sources of data and database software and more.

Successful Direct Marketing Methods
By Bob Stone
NTC Publishing Group, $49.95

Starting with the use of databases in marketing and going through strategic business planning and creativity and testing, this is as complete a guide to direct marketing as you'll find.

Winning Direct Response Advertising: From Print Through Interactive Media
By Joan Throckmorton
NTC Publishing, $49.95

A detailed and comprehensive treatise on what it takes to make effective direct response ads, including exercises, guidelines, and checklists for being creative; testing effectiveness and more.

Being Direct: Making Advertising Pay
By Lester Wunderman
Random House, $25.00

One of the most renowned direct marketers ever reveals what he has learned in six decades of working with Columbia Records, American Express, and other direct marketing organizations.

Periodicals

American Demographics
PO Box 10580
Riverton, NJ 08076–0580
Tel: (800) 529-7502
E-mail: subs@demographics.com
Web: www.demographics.com

A 75,000-circulation monthly magazine dedicated to providing news and information about markets, market research, direct marketing, databases, and related topics.

Catalog Age
11 River Bend Drive South
Stamford, CT 06907–0949
Tel: (203) 358-9900
Fax: (203) 358-5831
Web: www.catalogagemag.com

Covers news, trends, technologies and strategies for the catalog and e-commerce industries. It has a circulation of 14,000 and is published 13 times a year by Cowles Business Media.

DIRECT
11 River Bend Drive South
Stamford, CT 06907–0949
Tel: (203) 358-9900
Fax: (203) 358-5831
Web: www.directmag.com

Another Cowles Business Media publication that comes out 16 times a year for an audience of nearly 40,000 senior direct marketing executives. It covers just about every aspect of direct marketing, including postal and regulatory issues, creative, lists, customer relationship management and database marketing. It also reports on direct mail, telemarketing, e-mail, the Web, direct response television, alternative media, and new technology. There are also *DIRECT* Newsline, a daily online newsletter, and supplements on online marketing, teleservices, and business-to-business marketing.

Direct Marketing News
100 Avenue of the Americas
New York, NY 10013
Tel: (212) 925-7300
Fax: (212) 925-8752
Web: www.dmnews.com

A weekly print newspaper featuring news and information about virtually all aspects of direct marketing. It also offers three opt-in e-mail newsletters including *DM News Daily, CRM Weekly,* and *e-mail Marketing Weekly*; direct mail; telemarketing; and DRTV to Online Advertising, e-commerce and e-mail marketing. It has a controlled circulation of 40,000 catalogers, fundraisers, publishers, telemarketers, online marketers, database marketers, and others.

Sales and Marketing Management Magazine
70 Broadway
New York, NY 10003–9595
Tel: (646) 654-7259
E-mail:service@salesandmarketing.com
Web: www.salesandmarketing.com/smmnew

A monthly publication for senior-level executives in management of sales and marketing efforts. In addition to the monthly magazine with news and information, it produces *The Survey of Buying Power,* a reference guide to consumer purchasing trends.

Selling Power Magazine
1140 International Pkwy.
Fredericksburg, VA 22400
Tel: (800) 752-7355
Fax: (540) 752-7001
Web: www.sellingpower.com

Founded in 1986, this is a 200,000-circulation monthly providing information, news, and tips for sales managers.

Associations

American Association of Advertising Agencies
405 Lexington Avenue, 18th Floor
New York, NY 10174–1801
Tel: (212) 682-2500
Fax: (212) 682-8391
Web: www.aaaa.org

AAAA is the leading trade association for U.S. advertising agencies. It has a large collection of books and videotape for sale covering many different aspects of advertising.

American Management Association
1601 Broadway
New York, NY 10019
Tel: (212) 586-8100
Fax: (212) 903-8168
Web: www.amanet.org

The AMA is an international management development organization that sponsors seminars and conferences, publishes books and provides online resources.

American Marketing Association
311 S. Wacker Dr., Suite 5800
Chicago, IL 60606
Tel: (312) 542-9000
Fax: (312) 542-9001
Web: www.ama.org

The American Marketing Association is the leading professional society for marketers, holding workshops and seminars, publishing the biweekly magazine, *Marketing News*, offering certifications and providing online information and assistance.

American Teleservices Association
1620 I Street, NW, Suite 615
Washington, DC 20006
Tel: (202) 293-2452
Fax: (202) 463-8498
E-mail: ata@moinc.com
Web: www.ataconnect.org

A trade group for operators of call centers, trainers, consultants, equipment suppliers, and others in the telephone, Internet, and e-mail sales, service, and support industry. The organization provides telemarketers with education, technology updates, industry news, first-rate networking opportunities, and regulatory and legislative representation.

The Direct Marketing Association (DMA)
1120 Avenue of the Americas
New York, NY 10036–6700
Tel: (212) 768-7277
Fax: (212) 302-6714
Web: www.the-dma.org

Founded in 1917, it has 4,700 international members, making it the oldest and largest trade group for users and suppliers for users and suppliers in direct, database and interactive marketing. The

DMA lobbies regulators, provides education and information for members and performs other functions of a trade association.

Mailing & Fulfillment Service Association (MFSA)
1421 Prince Street
Alexandria, VA 22314–2806
Tel: (703) 836-9200
E-mail: mfsa-mail@MFSAnet.org
Web: www.masa.org

Formerly known as the Mail Advertising Service Association International, MFSA is a national trade association for the mailing and fulfillment services industry. Professional development, training, surveys, and government lobbying are among services it provides to its approximately 800 member companies.

National Mail Order Association
2807 Polk St. NE
Minneapolis, MN 55418–2954
Tel: (612) 788-1673
Fax: (612) 788-1147
Web: www.nmoa.org

Started in 1972, this organization aims to provide an information and contact clearinghouse for small to midsized businesses in mail-order marketing.

Pi Sigma Epsilon
6806 W. Wedgewood Drive
Milwaukee, WI 53220
Tel: (414) 328-1952
Fax: (414) 328-1953
E-mail: pse@pse.org
Web: www.pisigmaepsilon.org

A national professional fraternity in marketing, sales management, and selling, it was founded in 1952 and its members include college students, alumni, educators, and professional marketers. It provides education and assistance to students and others interested in entering marketing, sales, and sales management.

Sales & Marketing Executives-International, Inc. (SME)
P.O. Box 1390
Sumas, WA 98295–1390 USA
Tel: (770) 661-8500
Fax: (770) 661-8512
E-mail: smei@earthlink.net
Web: www.smei.org

SME dates its beginnings to 1935, when IBM founder Thomas Watson Sr. organized local sales manager clubs into a national organization. Today SME provides an online library of research and articles, a daily e-mail newsletter, and other services to CEOs, heads of marketing, and heads of sales in many countries.

Strategic Account Management Association
150 N. Wacker Dr., Suite 2222
Chicago, IL 60606
Tel: (312) 251-3131
Fax: (312) 251-3132
Web: www.nams.org

An international, nonprofit organization that provides 2,200 international members with training, conferences, books, CD-ROMs, and other resources, all related to the concept of customer-supplier partnering. It was established in 1964.

Western Fulfillment Management Association
P.O. Box 15281
North Hollywood, CA 91615
Tel: (310) 323-7220
Email: diggory1@aol.com
Web: www.wfma.org

An all-volunteer, informal nonprofit association for circulation professionals in the western United States. It provides an online job bank and sponsors meeting for its members.

Government Sources

Bureau of Labor Statistics
Division of Information Services
2 Massachusetts Avenue, N.E. Room 2860
Washington, DC 20212
Tel: (202) 691-5200
Fax: (202) 691-7890
Web: stats.bls.gov

The Department of Labor's Bureau of Labor Statistics is the source for a wide variety of data on labor economics and statistics about the American economy, from unemployment rates to hourly earnings. Among the most useful is the consumer expenditure survey data, available online at stats.bls.gov/csxhome.htm.

Census Bureau
4700 Silver Hill Road
Suitland, MD 20746
Tel: (301) 457-4608
Web: www.census.gov

The unit of the Commerce Department charged with counting American citizens, it also provides a wealth of economic and other business-related information of great value to marketers.

Fedworld
National Technical Information Service
Technology Administration
U.S. Department of Commerce
Springfield, VA 22161
Tel: (703) 605-6000
Web: www.fedworld.com

An online gateway to a vast array of federal government information available from many agencies through the Internet.

INDEX

D

N

O

P